APEX maths

4

Extension *for all* through problem solving

Teacher's Handbook
Year 4 / Primary 5

Paul Harrison

Ann Montague-Smith

CAMBRIDGE
UNIVERSITY PRESS

CAMBRIDGE UNIVERSITY PRESS
Cambridge, New York, Melbourne, Madrid, Cape Town, Singapore, São Paulo

Cambridge University Press
The Edinburgh Building, Cambridge CB2 2RU, UK

www.cambridge.org
Information on this title: www.cambridge.org/9780521754934

© Cambridge University Press 2003

First published 2003
Reprinted 2004, 2006

Printed in Dubai by Oriental Press

A catalogue record for this publication is available from the British Library

ISBN-13 978-0-521-75493-4 paperback
ISBN-10 0-521-75493-3 paperback

ACKNOWLEDGEMENTS
Content editing by Pete Crawford
Cover design by Karen Thomas
Cover photograph by John Walmsley
Text illustration by Rebecca Finn and Tom Morgan-Jones
Project management by Cambridge Publishing Management Limited
The authors and publishers would like to thank the schools and individuals who trialled lessons.

Contents

Introduction

Lesson plans

Introduction

About Apex Maths

Apex Maths uses problem solving to address the needs of the more able and also provides extension and enrichment opportunities for children of all abilities. This allows Apex Maths to be used within the context of the whole-class daily mathematics lesson, reflecting the philosophy of The National Numeracy Strategy *Framework for teaching mathematics*.

Thirty detailed lesson plans are presented in the Teacher's Handbook. Each focuses on a core problem or investigation that is differentiated in various ways so that children of all abilities can work at their level on the same basic problem.

The lessons address all the problem solving objectives in the *Framework* and span all the other *Framework* strands.

The problems are richer and deeper than the relatively straightforward word problems suggested in the *Framework*, thereby helping to develop thinking skills. They provide contexts in which children can apply and extend their mathematical skills and understanding, and consolidate their problem solving skills.

The teaching approach adopted throughout allows children to use enquiry, creative thinking and reasoning skills to solve a problem, with input from the teacher in the form of probing questions and occasional suggestions and hints. A carefully designed plenary encourages children to discuss their reasoning and evaluate the strategies used.

Teacher's materials

The Teacher's Handbook includes:

Scope and sequence chart
This lists all the problems together with the problem solving objectives addressed (from the *Framework for teaching mathematics*), the likely outcome levels for each ability group for Attainment Target 1 (Using and applying mathematics) in *The National Curriculum for England: mathematics* and the *Framework* topics addressed by each problem.

Scotland 5–14 Guidelines
A chart linking each lesson to related strands in *Curriculum and Assessment in Scotland, National Guidelines: Mathematics 5–14*.

Northern Ireland Lines of Development
A table linking each lesson to related *Northern Ireland Lines of Development* (levels 2 to 4).

Oral and mental problem solving starters
A bank of oral and mental starters with a problem solving slant, which can be used at the start of any lesson.

Lesson plans
These are presented in double page spreads. A blueprint on pages 8–9 explains the features of the plans. The lesson plans feature different types of problems, including:

- investigations requiring the identification of patterns and the making of generalisations;
- number puzzles and investigations that require reasoning about numbers;
- 'real-life' multi-stage problems involving a range of mathematics;
- word problems in which combinations of known values are used to find unknown values.

Useful mathematical information
This is a bank of additional mathematical information, perhaps explaining a particular concept or looking at a particular problem in greater depth.

Pupils' materials

Problems are presented for children in the Pupil's Textbook and/or using Photocopy Masters (PCMs) from the Teacher's Handbook. Sometimes differentiation of a problem involves giving clues or additional direction to the Average or Less able groups. Presenting a problem in two formats helps to avoid children using clues and directions intended for other ability groups.

Where parts of the page are numbered in the Textbook, this generally indicates a progression in the complexity of the problem. The Differentiation section in the Lesson plans indicates which parts of the pupil material are intended for which ability group.

Within the Textbook, an orange tinted box indicates text that all children should read.

Material for children to copy is tinted in light blue.

Equipment needed by children is shown in red text.

The Textbook also contains a glossary of mathematical and problem solving terms used in the problems.

Approaches to problem solving

When working at solving problems, children benefit from discussing what they have to do and how they might go about this. This can be as part of a whole-class discussion, or in pairs or small groups. On occasions, the discussion may not appear to be contributing to the resolution of the problem, but can be allowed to continue for a short while so that children gain confidence in putting forward their ideas and using mathematical vocabulary appropriately.

Problem solving offers excellent opportunities to develop thinking and reasoning skills. This should be encouraged so that children become confident in using these skills not just when involved in problem solving, but in all their mathematical work and in other curriculum areas. Children should be encouraged to:

- choose the appropriate mathematics for the problem, and explain why they made their choice;
- be confident to try different strategies, evaluate their effectiveness and recognise when their chosen strategy is not effective;
- draw a picture or diagram or use equipment to aid understanding;
- try a simpler case in order to understand how the problem could be solved;
- work in a systematic way, recording work in a logical order, so that it is clear to others what has been tried;

- look for a pattern;
- form hypotheses, asking and answering questions such as 'What if . . .?';
- consider if there are other, and better, solutions;
- try extensions to the problem, asking and answering 'What could I try next?';
- report what they have done in order to solve the problem, speaking clearly, and using appropriate mathematical vocabulary.

Because children approach problems from different perspectives, including different experiences of mathematics and varying degrees of understanding, it is important to accept a range of strategies for solving a problem and a variety of solutions. By making a comfortable atmosphere in which it is safe to put forward a view, idea or solution, children's confidence in their problem solving abilities will increase. It is also important to follow a problem through to a satisfactory solution, so that children can learn from others and improve their understanding of what is expected from them and ways of going about finding solutions. Expect your successes to improve as children's experience and confidence increases.

Sometimes when you ask a question, children will not respond immediately. Make use of silence; give children time to think through what has been asked so that they can formulate a response.

Lesson timing

The problem solving lessons in Apex Maths are designed to last for the length of a normal daily maths lesson. However, children's response to a given problem may determine whether the lesson could be extended for some minutes or returned to in another maths lesson.

Features of the lesson plans

Resources

Any Textbook pages, PCMs and equipment needed by the teacher, plus resources that children might choose to use, depending upon the problem solving approach they decide to take.

Key vocabulary

The main problem solving and mathematical terms associated with the problem.

What's the problem?

A brief description of the problem and the mathematics that might be encountered, bearing in mind that children may use different areas of mathematics to solve the problem in their own way.

Problem solving objectives

The key problem solving objectives for the lesson.

Differentiation

Suggested activities for different ability groups. Children should not feel restricted to one activity and should, where appropriate, be allowed to move on to a more demanding activity.

Introducing the problem

Ideas for introducing the problem to children before they consider their strategy and begin the investigation.

Minimum prior experience

The minimum mathematical experience required for children to participate in the lesson. This will help you to decide when in the year to use each lesson.

---

8 Number line race

Minimum prior experience

counting forwards and backwards, in steps of 2, 3 or 4, from any number (including negative numbers) on a number line

Resources

Textbook page 11, PCM 3, blank number lines

Key vocabulary

positive, negative, above/below zero, sequence, pattern, continue, number line

What's the problem?

Investigating sequences generated by counting on in equal steps along a number line, to find out which sequence generates a given number first. The investigation could involve calculating the difference between a negative and a positive number and dividing the difference.

Problem solving objectives

- Choose and use appropriate number operations and appropriate ways of calculating to solve problems.
- Explain methods and reasoning about numbers orally and in writing.
- Solve mathematical problems or puzzles, recognise and explain patterns and relationships, generalise and predict.

Differentiation

More able: Textbook page 11, problem 2 (range: –100 to 100; steps of 6, 9 and 11). There is also an extra challenge.

Average: Textbook page 11, problem 1 (range: –50 to 50; steps of 3, 4 and 6).

Less able: PCM 3 (range: –20 to 25; steps of 2, 3 and 4).

Differentiation will also be through methods used.

Introducing the problem

Draw a –10 to 10 number line. Invite children to count along it forwards and backwards in various constant steps, e.g.

- start at –1 and count forwards in 2s (–1, 1, 3, 5, 7, 9);
- start at 7 and count backwards in 3s (7, 4, 1, –2, –5, –8).

Repeat, with the whole class saying the numbers up to, say, 50 or –50.

Explain that the problems are about counting along a number line, but that it is actually possible to solve them without having to do any counting. Give children a few minutes to read through their problem and to ask any questions before they start.

Teacher focus for activity

All children: The majority of children will solve the problem by counting in the various steps and recording the numbers. As they do this, encourage them to identify and explain patterns that will assist them, e.g. with problem 2 on Textbook page 11, when counting in 9s from 19 to 91, the units digit decreases by 1 each time while the tens digit increases by 1. *Why is this?* (adding 9 is equivalent to adding 10 and subtracting 1)

You may need to point out that the number **after** the starting number is the result of the first jump – not the starting number itself.

More able and Average: Encourage children to record their work systematically. For each number in a sequence, they will need to know which jump number it was a result of. You could suggest that they devise a table of some sort to keep recordings manageable.

More able: Ask: *Is it possible to work out how many steps it takes to get from each start number to 100 without actually counting?*

Teacher focus for activity

Suggestions for facilitating the problem solving process and for developing children's problem solving skills as they work. It includes suggestions for probing questions, discussion points and areas to look out for.

Optional adult input

Provides a focus for assisting with particular groups if additional adult help is available.

Plenary

The main whole-class interactive teaching part of the lesson, with suggestions for discussion of solutions to the problem, the methods used, problem solving skills and the maths involved.

Development

Ideas for children to develop the problem, perhaps at home. They can also be used for children who manage to complete a problem early on in the lesson.

Solutions

Solutions to the problem at all levels for quick reference.

Useful mathematical information reference

A reference to indicate where you can find additional information about the mathematics involved in a problem.

Optional adult input

Work with the Average group. Discuss ways of recording jumps (e.g. on a number line or in a table).

Plenary

1 Ask children from each group to give their solutions and to describe their approach. Establish that one method of solving the problem is to work out the numbers that each frog landed on for each jump.

2 Discuss the ways in which children recorded the numbers. Establish that numbers need to be recorded carefully and that a table is an appropriate format. Draw a table similar to the one on PCM 3 as an example, or use one of the children's suggestions.

3 Read through PCM 3, establishing the starting numbers and jump size for each frog. Invite children to complete each row of the table

	start	1	2	3	4	5	6	7	8	9	10	11	12	13	14	15
							jump									
Fred	1	3	5	7	9	11	13	15	17	19	21	23	25			
Freda	−19	−15	−11	−7	−3	1	5	9	13	17	21	25				
Francis	−20	−17	−14	−11	−8	−5	−2	1	4	7	10	13	16	19	22	25

Discuss how, when counting on in negative integers, the numerical parts of the integers decrease in size. Ask children to identify any patterns they see, e.g. the odd numbers in Fred's row.

Establish that Freda reaches 25 first in 11 jumps; Fred is 1 jump behind; Francis is 4 jumps behind.

4 Deal with the Textbook problems in a similar way, generating similar tables (see **Useful mathematical information**, page 88) and the solutions:

● **Problem 1**

Fred reaches 50 first in 14 jumps. Freda and Francis are 6 jumps and 2 jumps behind him, respectively.

● **Problem 2**

Freda reaches 100 first in 14 jumps. Fred and Francis are 2 jumps and 4 jumps behind her, respectively.

An alternative method which the More able group may have suggested, or which you could introduce to them, is suggested in **Useful mathematical information**, pages 88–89.

Development

Children invent similar jumping frog problems for each other to solve, initially involving just 2 frogs.

Solutions

Textbook page 11

1 Fred reaches 50 first (14 jumps).
Freda is 6 jumps behind (20 jumps).
Francis is 2 jumps behind (16 jumps).

2 Freda arrives at 100 first (14 jumps).
Fred is 2 jumps behind (16 jumps).
Francis is 4 jumps behind (18 jumps).

Extra challenge: 64

PCM 3

Freda reaches 25 first (11 jumps).
Fred is 1 jump behind (12 jumps).
Francis is 4 jumps behind (15 jumps).

Lesson structure

Lessons have the recommended 3-part structure, but there is a slightly different emphasis on each part. As it is intended that children solve the problem in their own way, your input at the start of the activity is comparatively brief and is mainly concerned with introducing the problem and checking that children understand what is required.

The main teaching will take place indirectly, through probing questions, hints and suggestions as children work. Direct teaching takes place in the plenary, as solutions, problem solving methods and the mathematics involved are discussed. The plenary therefore contains much greater detail than the problem introduction. It offers opportunities for children to:

- use appropriate vocabulary;
- compare their strategies and solutions;
- listen to explanations, and develop their understanding, of mathematical ideas and strategies;
- ask and answer questions.

Differentiation

The problems in this book are differentiated in various ways:

- By level of difficulty

  Here there are different activities for different ability groups. Early finishers may be able to progress to an activity for a higher ability group.
- By outcome

  Here children are expected to approach the problem in more or less sophisticated ways, applying mathematical knowledge and understanding at their own level.
- By resource used as support

  Here children can choose different resources to support them, such as working mentally, using pencil and paper, using an empty number line or using a 100 square. Sometimes a hint may be provided for lower ability groups.
- By level of support

  Here, especially where additional adults are available, groups can be targeted for specific support.

Questioning techniques

There will be many opportunities to ask questions during a problem solving lesson.

Closed questions will give a response of yes or no, or elicit specific knowledge. They can be used to check understanding. Examples include:

- *Do you understand?* (yes/no)
- *What is half of three hundred?* (one hundred and fifty)

Open questions allow children the opportunity to give a range of responses. Examples include:

- *What fractions of what numbers can you think of that would give the answer of 60?* ($\frac{1}{2}$ of 120; $\frac{1}{4}$ of 240; $\frac{3}{4}$ of 80; $\frac{6}{10}$ of 100 . . .)
- *How could you solve this problem?*

Probing questions are nearly always open in the sense that they require a carefully thought out answer, where children decide how to explain their mathematics. These questions will give you the opportunity to assess their understanding. Examples include:

- *How did you work that out? Is there another way?*
- *What would happen if the numbers were changed to . . .? Would that make a difference? Why is that?*
- *Roughly what answer do you expect to get? How did you come to that estimate?*

Optional adult input

Children may need support and encouragement while they gain familiarity and confidence in working in a new way, or if they have limited experience of solving problems. You may find it helpful, if possible, to arrange for some additional classroom help, particularly when first using this resource.

There are suggestions in each lesson plan as to which group any additional adult could help with and in what way. Here are some general suggestions about how to make best use of an additional adult.

- Fully brief them about the problem for that lesson and what your expectations are for each ability group.
- Make sure that they understand that children should be allowed to solve a problem in their own way, even if at times it appears that they are going down a blind alley.
- Encourage use of suggested probing questions from the **Teacher focus for activity** section of each lesson. Also suggest the following 'catch all' questions:
- *Can you explain what you have done so far?*
- *Why did you do that?*
- *What are you going to do next?*

Class organisation

The lessons in Apex Maths have been specifically designed as whole-class numeracy lessons.

The differentiated ways in which the problems are presented make them ideal for mixed age classes. They are also highly suitable for schools where children are set by ability for mathematics lessons. The higher ability sets can work on the main problem and the average and lower ability sets can work on the differentiated presentations of the problem.

In mixed ability classes, children should be broadly grouped in the classroom according to ability. This will facilitate group discussion with the teacher if needed. It will also avoid children 'borrowing' clues or additional directions provided for children of a lesser ability.

Children should ideally work in pairs or threes when they are working on a problem or investigation. This will stimulate discussion – an essential component of the problem solving process.

Resources

Simple resources will be needed to support these activities, all of which are readily available. Some may be essential to the successful outcome of the activity. Others should be made available, so children can make decisions on resources needed.

General resources that may be useful, include:
- digit cards;
- individual whiteboards;
- number lines;
- 100 squares (PCM 8);
- multiplication squares;
- counters and centimetre cubes;
- squared paper (centimetre squares);
- calculators;
- pin boards (geoboards) and elastic bands;
- coins;
- tracing paper;
- small mirrors;
- place value boards.

Calculators

Some problem solving or investigatory procedures might involve many tedious or repetitious calculations that do not develop children's mathematical understanding. Others might involve calculations that are just beyond the ability of children who otherwise are making excellent progress towards solving the problem. In these cases, teachers should use their discretion as to whether to allow some children to use a calculator. In lessons in which this situation is likely to occur, 'calculators (discretionary)' is listed with the resources to be made available.

Assessment

While children are working at the problem, and during the plenary, target pairs and individuals in order to assess their skills in problem solving. Use probing questions, such as the examples given under **Questioning techniques**, and those given within the teacher's notes for the lesson. By targeting specific children during each problem solving lesson it is possible to ensure that all children will be assessed through discussion over time.

Look for signs of consistency in approach to a given problem. Make sure that children read all of the data and are able to sort which data is relevant and which should be discarded.

When discussing their work, take the opportunity to identify whether children have understood the mathematics involved. This is an ideal time to check whether there are any misconceptions that need remedying.

Watch for children who rely too heavily upon their partner for:
- how to solve the problem

  Does the child understand what the problem involves?
- mathematical calculations

  Does the child understand which calculation strategies and procedures to use, and can they use these themselves?
- recording the problem

  Is the child able to suggest how the results might be presented?
- answering open and probing questions and reporting back in the plenary

  Is the child able to articulate their thinking? Does the child have the appropriate vocabulary and can they use it appropriately to express mathematical ideas and explanations? Are they given enough response time?

During the problem solving lesson take time to stand back and observe what the children are doing:
- Do children cooperate?
- Are they working collaboratively?
- Do they both contribute to the discussion, or does one dominate, taking the lead?
- Do they use appropriate mathematical language in order to express their ideas?

Scope and sequence chart

This lists all the problems together with:

- the problem solving objectives addressed (from the *NNS Framework for teaching mathematics*);
- the likely outcome levels for each ability group for Attainment Target 1 (Using and applying mathematics) in *The National Curriculum for England: mathematics;*
- the *Framework* topics addressed by each problem.

Because children will solve problems in different ways, using different aspect of mathematics, the specific *Framework* objectives that will be addressed will vary. For this reason, only the topics that are likely to be addressed have been referenced.

* Indicates that the general mathematical content may extend the Most able beyond the Year 4 objectives in the *Framework for teaching mathematics.*

Problem	Problem solving objectives involved					Ma1 Using and applying mathematics Level/Outcome			Mathematical topics
	Choose and use appropriate operations and appropriate ways of calculating …	Explain methods and reasoning about numbers orally and in writing.	Solve mathematical problems or puzzles, recognise and explain patterns …	Make and investigate a general statement about familiar numbers or shapes …	Use all four operations to solve word problems involving numbers in 'real life', money and measures …	More able	Average	Less able	
1 What are we?*		■	■			Level 3/4	Level 3	Level 2/3	Place value, ordering and rounding (whole numbers) Properties of numbers and number sequences Mental calculation strategies (+ and −)
2 Sum puzzle		■	■			Level 4	Level 3/4	Level 3	Mental calculation strategies (+ and −)
3 Animal farm*	■	■	■			Level 4	Level 3/4	Level 3	Fractions and decimals Rapid recall of × and ÷ facts Mental calculation strategies (+, −, × and ÷)
4 Money bags		■	■			Level 4	Level 3/4	Level 3	Properties of numbers and number sequences Mental calculation strategies (+ and −)
5 Computer crash!*		■	■			Level 4	Level 3/4	Level 3	Mental calculation strategies (+ and −)
6 Sponsored walk*	■	■			■	Level 4	Level 3/4	Level 2/3	Mental calculation strategies (+, −, × and ÷) Pencil and paper procedures (+, −, × and ÷) Understanding × and ÷
7 Shape mobiles*	■	■	■			Level 4	Level 3/4	Level 3	Properties of numbers and number sequences Mental calculation strategies (+, −, × and ÷) Rapid recall of × and ÷ facts Shape and space

Problem	Problem solving objectives involved					Ma1 Using and applying mathematics Level/Outcome More able	Average	Less able	Mathematical topics
8 Number line race*	■	■	■			Level 4/5	Level 3/4	Level 2/3	Place value, ordering and rounding (whole numbers) Properties of numbers and number sequences Mental calculation strategies (+, −, × and ÷)
9 Fair shares*		■	■			Level 4	Level 3/4	Level 3	Properties of numbers and number sequences Fractions and decimals Mental calculation strategies (+ and −)
10 Puzzling symbols*	■	■	■			Level 4	Level 3/4	Level 3	Understanding + and − Mental calculation strategies (+, −, × and ÷) Understanding × and ÷
11 Seating arrangements	■	■	■			Level 4	Level 3/4	Level 2/3	Properties of numbers and number sequences Mental calculation strategies (+, −, × and ÷)
12 Secret code			■			Level 4	Level 3/4	Level 2/3	Properties of numbers and number sequences Shape and space
13 Palindromic investigation*	■	■	■			Level 4	Level 3/4	Level 2/3	Mental calculation strategies (+ and −) Pencil and paper procedures (+ and −)
14 Windows			■			Level 4	Level 3/4	Level 3	Shape and space
15 Number neighbours*	■		■	■		Level 4	Level 3/4	Level 3	Properties of numbers and number sequences Mental calculation strategies (+, −, × and ÷)
16 PE purchases*	■	■			■	Level 4	Level 3/4	Level 2/3	Mental calculation strategies (+, −, × and ÷) Pencil and paper procedures (+, −, × and ÷)
17 Area challenge			■			Level 4	Level 3/4	Level 3	Measures Shape and space
18 Dog run		■	■	■		Level 4/5	Level 3/4	Level 3	Shape and space
19 Ginger biscuits*	■	■			■	Level 4	Level 3/4	Level 2/3	Mental calculation strategies (+, −, × and ÷) Pencil and paper procedures (+, −, × and ÷)
20 Wristbands		■	■			Level 4	Level 3/4	Level 2/3	Properties of numbers and number sequences
21 Grid totals		■	■	■		Level 3/4	Level 3	Level 2/3	Understanding + and − Mental calculation strategies (+ and −)
22 Quick time	■	■	■		■	Level 4	Level 3/4	Level 3	Mental calculation strategies (+, −, × and ÷) Measures
23 Winning totals	■	■	■			Level 4	Level 3/4	Level 2/3	Properties of numbers and number sequences Mental calculation strategies (+, −, × and ÷) Rapid recall of × and ÷ facts

Problem	Problem solving objectives involved					Ma1 Using and applying mathematics Level/Outcome			Mathematical topics
						More able	Average	Less able	
24 Colourful cars*	■	■			■	Level 4	Level 3/4	Level 3	Fractions and decimals Organising and interpreting data Mental calculation strategies (+, −, × and ÷)
25 Test ramp*	■	■			■	Level 4	Level 3/4	Level 3	Fractions and decimals Mental calculation strategies (+, −, × and ÷) Measures
26 The Pizza Place*	■	■	■			Level 4/5	Level 4	Level 2/3	Fractions and decimals Understanding × and ÷ Mental calculation strategies (+ and −)
27 Tangrams			■			Level 4	Level 3	Level 2/3	Shape and space
28 Last digit patterns*			■	■		Level 4/5	Level 3/4	Level 3	Properties of numbers and number sequences Rapid recall of × and ÷ facts Shape and space
29 Ruritanian Lotto*		■	■	■		Level 4	Level 3/4	Level 3	Place value, ordering and rounding (whole numbers) Mental calculation strategies (+ and −)
30 Cutting the cake*	■	■	■			Level 4/5	Level 3/4	Level 3	Mental calculation strategies (+ and −) Fractions and decimals

	Problem solving and enquiry	Information handling	Range and type of numbers	Money	Add and subtract	Multiply and divide	Fractions, percentages and ratio	Patterns and sequences	Functions and equations	Measure and estimate	Time	Shape, position and movement
1 What are we?	●		●		●			●				
2 Sum puzzle	●				●				●			
3 Animal farm	●				●	●	●					
4 Money bags	●			●	●			●				
5 Computer crash!	●				●							
6 Sponsored walk	●			●	●	●	●					
7 Shape mobiles	●				●	●						●
8 Number line race	●		●		●			●				
9 Fair shares	●				●		●					
10 Puzzling symbols	●				●	●			●			
11 Seating arrangements	●				●	●		●				
12 Secret code	●							●				●
13 Palindromic investigation	●				●							
14 Windows	●											●
15 Number neighbours	●				●	●		●				
16 PE purchases	●			●	●	●						
17 Area challenge	●									●		●
18 Dog run	●							●				●
19 Ginger biscuits	●			●	●	●						
20 Wristbands	●							●				
21 Grid totals	●				●							
22 Quick time	●				●	●					●	
23 Winning totals	●				●	●						
24 Colourful cars	●	●			●	●						
25 Test ramp	●				●	●	●			●		
26 The Pizza Place	●					●	●					
27 Tangrams	●											●
28 Last digit patterns	●					●		●				●
29 Ruritanian Lotto	●		●		●			●				
30 Cutting the cake	●				●		●					

In each activity, children will need to employ the three problem-solving steps of (1) starting, (2) doing and (3) reporting on a task. Encourage children to choose appropriate strategies at each stage, and to evaluate their choices.

Northern Ireland Lines of Development (Levels 2 to 4)

'Processes in mathematics' applies to all lessons.

	Lesson	Related Lines of Development
1	What are we?	N2.6, N3.1, N4.1, R2.5
2	Sum puzzle	HD3.4, N4.3
3	Animal farm	N3.4, N3.12, N3.16, N4.3
4	Money bags	N2.6, N3.4, R3.4, R4.3
5	Computer crash!	N2.6, N3.4, N4.3
6	Sponsored walk	N3.15, N4.18
7	Shape mobiles	N3.4, N3.12, N4.3, S2.3, S3.2
8	Number line race	N3.14, N5.3, R4.3
9	Fair shares	N2.6, N2.8, N3.4, N3.16, N3.18
10	Puzzling symbols	N2.6, N2.8, N3.3, N3.4, N3.17, N4.12, R2.6
11	Seating arrangements	N2.6, N3.4, N4.3, R3.4
12	Secret code	R3.4
13	Palindromic investigation	N3.5, N4.2
14	Windows	S3.5, S3.6
15	Number neighbours	N2.6, N3.4, N3.14, N4.3, N4.12
16	PE purchases	N3.15, N4.18
17	Area challenge	A4.1, A4.2, S3.4
18	Dog run	R3.4, S2.3, S3.7
19	Ginger biscuits	N3.15, N4.10, N4.18
20	Wristbands	N3.22, N3.23, R4.4
21	Grid totals	N2.2, N2.5, N2.6
22	Quick time	T3.1, T3.3, T4.1
23	Winning totals	N2.6, N3.4, N3.12
24	Colourful cars	N2.5, N2.6, N3.4, N3.14, N3.16, HD3.3
25	Test ramp	M3.5, M4.4, M4.13, N3.4, N3.14, N3.16, N4.12
26	The Pizza Place	N3.14, N3.16, N3.17, N3.18, R3.5
27	Tangrams	S3.6
28	Last digit patterns	N3.12, R3.4, S3.5
29	Ruritanian Lotto	N2.6, N3.1, N4.1, R3.4
30	Cutting the cake	N2.6, N3.16

Oral and mental problem solving starters

Oral and mental activities for the start of each lesson can be selected from this bank of problem solving starters or from other sources.

Children could show their answers using digit cards or fans, individual whiteboards or scraps of paper. This allows less confident children to attempt answers without fear of being incorrect in front of others. It also enables you to survey all children's answers, making a note of common errors or responses from particular individuals.

Allow children time to think about a problem before you expect an answer. You could ask them to wait for a signal from you before they show their answers. This allows all children an equal opportunity to answer questions, not just the quicker or more confident ones.

1 What am I?

(place value)

Children will need scrap paper or individual whiteboards for their workings. Write clues on the board:

- I'm a 2-digit number less than 20.
  The sum of my digits is 8.
  What am I? (17)
- I'm a 3-digit number.
  The sum of my digits is 4.
  2 of my digits are the same.
  My hundreds digit is double my tens digit.
  What am I? (211)
- I'm a 4-digit multiple of 10 between 1000 and 2000.
  The sum of my digits is 6.
  None of my digits are the same.
  My tens digits is bigger than my hundreds digit.
  What am I? (1230)
- I'm a 4-digit number less than 4000.
  All my digits are odd.
  My tens digit is the same as my units digit.
  My hundreds digit is 2 less than my thousands digit.
  The sum of my digits is 14.
  What am I? (3155)

After each problem, discuss children's reasoning.

2 Make 5

(mental calculation strategies)

Children make 5 using the four operations, e.g. (with operations carried out in order)

$$5 \times 3 + 5 \div 4 \text{ and } 2 + 16 \div 3 - 1$$

Children explain their solution verbally rather than writing it down. Repeat for other numbers such as 10. Opportunity will arise to discuss the inverse relationship between addition and subtraction and between multiplication and division (i.e. one operation 'undoes' the other).

3 Multiple pairs

(properties of numbers; mental calculation strategies (+ and −))

Write these numbers:

15   16   19   23   25   28   32   47   64   91

Invite children to add numbers to make multiples of 10 using each number no more than once. How many different multiples of 10 can the class make? Children will probably start by adding pairs of numbers but should soon realise that combining two or more pairs of numbers will create further multiples of 10.

4 Giving change

(mental calculation strategies (+ and −) with money)

Give the price of an item and the money given to buy it. Children work out the change using the fewest coins possible, e.g.

- I buy a cake for £2.35. I give £3. (change: 50p, 10p, 5p)
- I buy a ball for £2.96. I give £4. (change: £1, 2p, 2p)
- I buy a CD for £12.75. I give £15. (change: £2, 20p, 5p)
- I buy a cap for £3.39. I give £10. (change: £5, £1, 50p, 10p, 1p)
- I buy a pencil for 7p. I give 50p. (change: 20p, 20p, 2p, 1p)

Discuss the methods children use for finding the amount of change and for working out the coins to use.

5 All the sums (and differences)

(mental calculation strategies (+ and −))

Write 4 numbers. Allow children about a minute to write down as many totals as they can using two or more of the numbers. Children then show their totals. Write them on the board.

> 15, 5, 16, 21 (possible totals: 20, 21, 26, 31, 36, 37, 41, 42, 52, 57)

Congratulate children who found all the totals and ask them to explain their procedures for finding them all. Recommend procedures that are systematic. Discuss methods of addition.

Children can also find all possible differences. (For the numbers above, these are 1, 5, 6, 10, 11, 16.)

6 What's the fraction?

(fractions)

Ask children to work out what fraction one number is of another, e.g.

What fraction of . . .

- *50 is 25?* $(\frac{1}{2})$
- *6 is 2?* $(\frac{1}{3})$
- *60 is 20?* $(\frac{1}{3})$
- *12 is 3?* $(\frac{1}{4})$
- *100 is 10?* $(\frac{1}{10})$
- *16 is 2?* $(\frac{1}{8})$
- *20 is 4?* $(\frac{1}{5})$

Discuss the methods children use. Essentially they involve dividing the smaller number into the larger, but children may have different ways of doing this.

Initially use only numbers that involve unit fractions and make sure that the numbers are within the capabilities of children. For more able children, you could occasionally introduce numbers that involve non-unit fractions such as $\frac{3}{4}$, $\frac{2}{3}$ or $\frac{6}{10}$, e.g.

- *What fraction of 60 is 45?* $(\frac{3}{4})$
- *What fraction of 12 is 8?* $(\frac{2}{3})$
- *What fraction of 50 is 30?* $(\frac{6}{10})$

7 Different rectangles

(shape and space)

Draw 3 lines of different lengths to represent straws (or geostrips). Label them A, B and C.

- *How many different rectangles (including squares) can I make with straws of three different lengths?*

A   B   C

Children work in pairs, recording the different rectangles in their own way. Allow a minute or so before inviting children to give their results. Discuss children's methods of recording, e.g. sketching the rectangles or using the letters A, B and C. Establish that there are 6 different rectangles (including squares) using straws as follows: 2 As and 2 Bs; 2 As and 2 Cs; 2 Bs and 2 Cs; 4 As; 4 Bs; 4 Cs.

8 Will I say . . .?

(ordering)

I'm counting back on a number line . . .

- *I'm counting back in 2s from 12. Will I say negative 2? (yes)*
- *I'm counting back in 3s from 30. Will I say zero? (yes)*
- *I'm counting back in 2s from 15. Will I say negative 2? (no)*
- *I'm counting back in 5s from 12. Will I say negative 3? (yes)*
- *I'm counting back in 3s from 7. Will I say negative 10? (no)*

After each question and its responses, ask children to explain how they arrived at their answer. Encourage children to reason about numbers rather than merely counting back, e.g. with the first question, reasoning that when counting back in steps of 2 from an even number, 'zero' will be said, so 'negative 2' (one more step back) will be said. Children confirm answers by counting back.

9 All the multiplications

(mental calculation strategies (× and ÷); rapid recall of multiplication and division facts)

Invite children to give you as many multiplications as they can, each with a product of 24. Write each multiplication on the board. Initially these are likely to be facts from multiplication tables. Encourage children to use known facts to find others, e.g. knowing that $6 \times 4 = 24$, deducing that $4 \times 6 = 24$, and then halving one number and doubling the other to produce $2 \times 12 = 24$. Have children considered multiplying more than two numbers, e.g. $2 \times 3 \times 4 = 24$?

Repeat with other 'factor-rich' numbers such as 36 and 60.

10 Number neighbours

(mental calculation strategies (+ and −))

Give the sums of consecutive numbers. (Ensure the sums are always odd.) Children work out what the numbers could be. For example:

- *The sum of two consecutive numbers (number neighbours) is 17. What are the numbers? (8 and 9)*

● *The sum of two consecutive numbers is 55. What are the numbers?* (27 and 28)

Discuss children's strategies.

11 Show me a number

(properties of numbers and number sequences)

Give some properties of a number. Children give a number with those properties. For example:

Show me . . .

● *a multiple of 3 between 20 and 30 that is odd.* (21 or 27)

● *a multiple of 5 between 20 and 100 that is even.*
(30, 40, 50, 60, 70, 80 or 90)

● *a multiple of both 2 and 3 between 20 and 50.*
(24, 30, 36, 42 or 48)

● *an odd multiple of 5 between 30 and 70.* (35, 45, 55 or 65)

● *a 2-digit multiple of 4 that is also divisible by 10.*
(20, 40, 60 or 80)

Discuss children's reasoning.

12 Venn sort

(handling data)

Draw this Venn diagram.

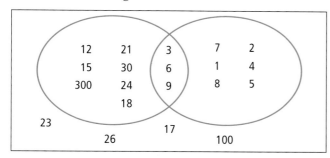

Secretly allocate each ring a number property, e.g. 'multiple of 3' and '1-digit'. Slowly enter a variety of numbers into the different sections of the diagram (including outside the rings) according to the two properties. Children indicate when they think they know what the property of each ring is.

Other pairs of properties that could be used are:

● multiple of 2; multiple of 3

● odd; less than 20

● multiple of 10; 2 digits

● multiple of 5; odd

13 Television time

(measures (time); mental calculation strategies (+ and −))

Give word problems involving time in the context of television, e.g.

● *Jack watched a television programme from 6:27 to 7 o'clock. How long was the programme?* (33 minutes)

● *One television programme lasted 38 minutes and another lasted 55 minutes. What was the total length of the two programmes in hours and minutes?* (1 hour and 33 minutes)

● *Two programmes were recorded onto a 2-hour videotape. One programme was 50 minutes long; the other was 45 minutes long. How much time was left on the videotape?* (25 minutes)

● *A programme finished at 5:55. It had been on for 1 hour 30 minutes. When did it start?* (4:25)

● *Because of the football final all programmes are running 33 minutes late. What time will a programme scheduled to start at 3:45 now start?* (4:18)

Discuss methods of calculation.

14 Place the digits

(mental calculation strategies)

Write the digits 1, 2, 3 and 4 and this calculation format: ✱✱ + ✱✱ = 55

Children use all of the digits 1, 2, 3 and 4 to replace the ✱s.

Discuss the possible solutions (21 + 34; 34 + 21; 24 + 31; 31 + 24) and how children tackled the problem.

Repeat with other formats, e.g.

✱ × ✱ + ✱✱ = 24	(3 × 4 + 12 = 24)
✱✱ ÷ ✱ + ✱ = 8	(12 ÷ 3 + 4 = 8)
✱✱ − ✱✱ = 11	(24 − 13 = 11)
✱ × ✱ + ✱✱ = 20	(3 × 2 + 14 = 20)
✱✱ ÷ ✱ + ✱ = 10	(14 ÷ 2 + 3 = 10)
✱✱ ÷ ✱ − ✱ = 16	(34 ÷ 2 − 1 = 16)
✱✱ ÷ ✱ + ✱ = 15	(42 ÷ 3 + 1 = 15)

Invite children to make up their own formats. Use different digits.

15 Make the measure

(measures; fractions and decimals)

Give a target mass such as 2 kg. Invite children to give two masses that equal it, e.g. 1 kg and 1 kg; 1.5 kg and 0.5 kg; 1 kg 600 g and 400 g. Repeat with other masses. Periodically introduce a condition, e.g.

- all answers in grams;
- all answers in kilograms;
- all answers in kilograms and grams;
- one answer in kilograms and the other in grams;
- answers using fractions.

The activity can be adapted for length and capacity.

16 Hexagon shapes

(shape and space)

Display one or more large regular hexagons (on paper, on the board or preferably using an overhead projector). Provide children with several outlines of hexagons for sketching their ideas on.

Ask children how vertices of the hexagon can be joined to make various shapes. For each shape they use their hexagons as an aid to sketch on and indicate when they have made the shape. Invite children to show their solution on the display shape. Encourage children to find more than one example of each shape. Shapes could include: isosceles, right-angled, equilateral and scalene (i.e. no 2 sides equal) triangles; rectangle; quadrilateral; pentagon.

These are just some examples of how vertices can be joined:

17 Target 100

(mental calculation strategies (+ and −))

Say: *Give me two numbers with a total of 100.*

Ask children to explain the strategy they used for finding the numbers. Initially numbers are likely to be multiples of 10 or a 1-digit and a 2-digit number. After a time, introduce conditions such as 'no multiples of 10', 'no multiples of 5' or 'no 1-digit numbers'.

18 What could I be?

(numbers and the number system)

Pick a child to start. They secretly write any number, say 64, on a scrap of paper or individual whiteboard, round it to the nearest 10 and say: *Rounded to the nearest 10, I am* (in this example) *60. What could I be?* Children then show what they think the number is (55, 56, 57, 58, 59, 60, 61, 62, 63 or 64). The secret number is then revealed. Choose a child with the correct answer (or the nearest to it) to choose the next secret number.

The activity can be extended to include rounding to 100 and rounding a sum of money to the nearest 10p or pound.

19 Sums, differences and products

(mental calculation strategies)

Give information on the product, sum or difference of a pair of numbers or some other relationship between them. Children work out what the numbers are. Occasionally discuss methods of solution. Here are some examples:

- *The sum is 12 and the difference is 8.* (2 and 10)
- *The sum is 15 and the product is 50.* (5 and 10)
- *The product is 36 and the difference is 5.* (9 and 4)
- *The product is 18 and one number is twice as big as the other.* (3 and 6)
- *The product is 500 and the difference is 40.* (10 and 50)

20 Linked shapes

(shape and space)

Work around the class. One child starts by naming a shape. Each child in turn names a shape that is linked to the previous shape in some way and describes the link, e.g. square, rectangle (both have 4 sides), right-angled triangle (both have a right angle), scalene triangle (both have 3 sides), irregular hexagon (both are irregular), regular hexagon (both have 6 sides) . . . Look out for too many repetitions of particular shapes, encouraging children to use new shapes wherever possible. Continue until the links become exhausted or tenuous.

21 Ordered fractions

(fractions and decimals)

Write fractions and decimals (up to 1) on a set of 10 or more large cards or pieces of paper. Shuffle and stack the cards. Invite a child to pick up the top card and stand in front of the class with the number showing. Invite other children, one at a time, to pick up the next top card and position themselves with children already at the front, so the fractions and decimals are in order, smallest to largest from left to right. Ask children to explain the reasons for their positioning. Encourage the rest of the class to indicate if they disagree with the positioning and to give their reasons.

22 Too big, too small

(ordering)

Write a number range on the board, e.g. 0 to 100. One child thinks of a number within the range. The other children try to guess what it is. The response from the first child can only be 'too big' or 'too small'. The child who guesses correctly thinks of the next number.

After a few rounds ask if children can think of a good strategy for working out the number with the fewest number of guesses, e.g. first asking if the number is 50, then if it is 25 or 75, depending upon the response to the first guess; and gradually cutting the range of possibilities by half each time, 'homing in' on the number.

23 The answer to the question

(fractions)

Say: *The answer to the question is one tenth. What is the question?*

Encourage children to be imaginative and think of a range of questions in all areas of mathematics, e.g.

- What fraction of a pound is 10p?
- What fraction of a metre is 10 centimetres?
- What fraction of a 100 square is one row?
- What fraction of 200 is 20?
- What is 0.1 as a fraction?
- What fraction is $\frac{10}{100}$ equivalent to?
- What fraction of all the toes on your feet is one toe?
- If you divide a rectangle into 10 equal parts what fraction is each part?
- If you divide a shape into 20 equal parts what fraction is 2 parts?

You could use other fractions.

24 How many fives?

(place value)

Say: *How many times is the digit '5' used in numbers from 1 to 100?*

Allow children up to a minute to work this out. Discuss their methods, e.g. reasoning that there are 10 '5' units digits (in 5, 15, 25 . . . 95) and another 10 '5' tens digits (in 50, 51, 52 . . . 59), making 20 '5' digits altogether.

- *How many times is the digit '0' used?* (11, including both zeros of 100)
- *How many times is the '5' used in numbers from 500 to 599?* (120)

Discuss methods.

25 Multiplication grid

(rapid recall of multiplication and division facts)

Draw this incomplete multiplication grid.

Explain that each number in the table is the product of the number in the left column and the number in the top row.

×		2	5
		8	20
3		6	
	15		50
			20

Invite children to help you complete the table. Children indicate when they think they know the number for a particular square. Each time, ask children to justify their number. (The numbers in the top row are 3, 2, 5 and 10 and those down the left column are 4, 3, 5 and 2.)

Repeat with other grids.

26 Brick calculations

(mental calculation strategies (+ and −))

Draw this format, but only write the numbers on the bottom row of bricks. Explain that each brick has a number that is the sum of the numbers of the two bricks supporting it. Ask children to help you complete the other bricks.

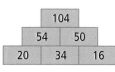

Rub the numbers out and just enter 50 in the top brick. Children work in pairs to find as many different combinations as they can for the bottom row that will give the top total. Allow about 2 minutes for this, then share children's solutions.

Use other numbers in the top brick.

27 Target 50

(mental calculations)

Write 50, 2, 5, 10, + and ×.

Explain to the class that their challenge is to reach the target of 50 using the numbers 2, 5 and 10, and multiplication and addition in as many ways as they can. They can use the numbers as many times as they like in each calculation.

When they are ready, invite children to write their suggested calculations on the board. Help them to use brackets where necessary for clarity. Ask children to explain their methods of calculation. Here are some possible expressions:

$5 \times 10 = 50$

$(10 \times 2) + (10 \times 2) + 10 = 50$

$2 \times 5 \times 5 = 50$

$(5 \times 5) + (5 \times 5) = 50$

$(2 \times 2 \times 5) + (2 \times 2 \times 5) + (2 \times 5) = 50$

28 Dartboard

(mental calculation strategies)

Draw this dartboard.

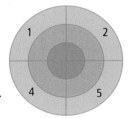

Explain that the outer ring is worth just the number; the middle ring is worth the number doubled; the inner ring is worth the number trebled. Give children a number. They must try and achieve the number in different ways using exactly 3 darts (all darts must land on the board). List all the different ways on the board. For example, 30 can be achieved with:

● 2 treble 4s and a double 3;

● 2 treble 3s and a treble 4;

● 1 treble 2 and 2 treble 4s.

Another approach is to try to make each of the numbers 1 to 36 (the maximum possible) in order.

Use other numbers on the dartboard.

29 What's the division?

(mental calculation strategies (× and ÷))

Write 1, 2, 3 and 4 and this division format:

Ask children to use the digits 1, 2, 3 and 4 in the digit boxes in as many ways as they can so that a remainder of 1 results. Each digit can be used only once in each division. Possibilities are:

$13 \div 2 = 6$ remainder 1
$31 \div 2 = 15$ remainder 1
$41 \div 2 = 20$ remainder 1
$43 \div 2 = 21$ remainder 1
$13 \div 4 = 3$ remainder 1
$21 \div 4 = 5$ remainder 1

Repeat for remainders of 2, 3 and 0.

The activity can be done using different digits, e.g. 2, 3, 4 and 5.

30 Make a sequence

(properties of numbers and number sequences)

Write a pair of numbers and ask children to create a sequence of numbers that includes them. For example, if the two numbers are 3 and 15, examples of sequences that include them are:

$...1\ 3\ 5\ 7\ 9\ 11\ 13\ \mathbf{15}\ 17\ 19...$ (odd numbers)
$...3\ 7\ 11\ \mathbf{15}\ 19...$ (add 4)
$3\ 6\ 9\ 12\ \mathbf{15}\ 18...$ (multiples of 3)
$3\ 9\ \mathbf{15}\ 21...$ (add 6)

Extend the activity to include a negative number as one of the pair.

Lesson plans

1 What are we?

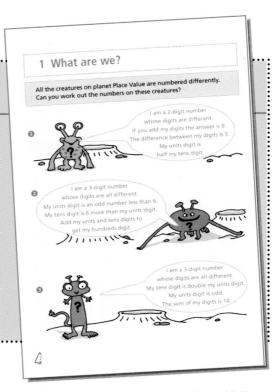

Minimum prior experience

place value in 3-digit numbers; mental calculation with single digits; understanding of 'odd' and 'even'

Resources

Textbook pages 2 and 3

Key vocabulary

digit, one-, two-, three-, four-digit number, units, tens, hundreds, thousands, ten thousands, place, place value, odd, even

What's the problem?

Children use clues about digits to find unknown numbers of up to 5 digits. Problems mainly require reasoning about numbers, but also involve simple calculations and knowledge of odd and even numbers.

Problem solving objectives

- Explain methods and reasoning about numbers orally and in writing.
- Solve mathematical problems or puzzles, recognise and explain patterns and relationships, generalise and predict. Suggest extensions by asking 'What if . . .?'

Differentiation

More able: Textbook page 3, problems 5 and 6 (problems based on 4- and 5-digit numbers).

Average: Textbook pages 2 and 3, problems 3 and 4 (similar problems but based on 3- and 4-digit numbers).

Less able: Textbook page 2, problems 1 and 2 (similar problems but based on 2- and 3-digit numbers).

Introducing the problem

Write the number 52 460. Ask children to identify the value

TTh	Th	H	T	U
5	2	4	6	0

of each place in the number. Write an abbreviation of each place value above the digits.

Discuss the value of each digit, e.g. the value of the '4' is four hundred.

Explain that children will be solving number riddles where they work out what numbers are from clues about their digits. Encourage them to read through all the clues before they start a problem.

Teacher focus for activity

More able and Average: Encourage children to look for a clue that will give them a starting point, e.g. in problem 3, 'My units digit is odd' will provide the possibilities of 1, 3, 5, 7 or 9 in the units place.

Discuss ways of keeping work orderly, e.g. using several sets of digit boxes in which to record all possibilities for the digits in each number.

Asking children to justify the positioning of digits will indicate whether they are reasoning about numbers or merely guessing.

When children arrive at a solution, encourage them to check it against the clues.

Less able: Problems 1 and 2 can be solved by working through the clues in order. Ask children to say what possibilities each clue generates. You may need to point out that where a calculation for a digit results in a number greater than 9, that possibility can be discarded.

Optional adult input

Work with the Average group. As children work, ask them to give reasons for placing digits where they have. Ask them to check that the digits fit the clues.

Plenary

1   Invite children to give you their answers for each problem. Confirm the correct answers.

Select one or two of the problems and ask children to explain briefly the methods they used. Emphasise that:

- clues may be used in a different order to which they are presented;

- methods that are systematic (rather than random trials) are quicker and involve less work (are more efficient).

2   Read through problem 4. Establish from the first clue that the number has four digits that are all different. Elicit that a 4-digit number has places for thousands, hundreds, tens and units.

Ask: *What clue could we start with?*

Discuss children's responses. Establish that the second or third clues provide enough information to get started and that the last clue is not helpful at this stage.

Ask: *How could we use the second and third clues?*

Discussions are likely to be along the following lines:

- From the first part of the second clue (the units digit is double the thousands digit), the units digit must be must be 0, 2, 4, 6 or 8. (Discuss the fact that any number doubled is an even number.) To produce these possibilities, the thousands digit must be 0, 1, 2, 3 or 4.

- Elicit that zeros can be discounted, as they are not normally used at the start of a whole number. (Discuss the reason for this: a zero is a place holder and so has no useful purpose at the beginning of a number.)

Write the current possibilities:

Th	H	T	U
1			2

Th	H	T	U
2			4

Th	H	T	U
3			6

Th	H	T	U
4			8

However, the third clue tells us that the thousands digit is odd, so we can discard numbers with 2 or 4 in the thousands place. So the possibilities are now narrowed to:

Th	H	T	U
1			2

Th	H	T	U
3			6

The second clue also tells us that the units digit is one less than the tens digit, so we can enter the possibilities for the tens digit:

Th	H	T	U
1		3	2

Th	H	T	U
3		7	6

Ask: *How does the final clue help us?*

The final clue tells us that the hundreds digit is the difference between the tens and the thousands digits.

In the first possibility above, the difference between the two digits is 2, but 2 has already been used for the units digit.

In the second possibility, the difference is 4. So the solution is 3476.

Invite children to check this number against the clues.

Possible approaches to all the other problems are provided in **Useful mathematical information**, pages 84–85.

Development

Children make up similar riddles, ensuring there is only one possible solution.

Solutions

1 63   2 871

3 563   4 3476

5 9643
6 23 654 and 34 976 (if the ten thousands digit is odd)

2 Sum puzzle

Minimum prior experience

mental addition of 3 single-digit numbers

Resources

Textbook page 4, small pieces of card, digit cards

Key vocabulary

add, addition, sum, total, plus, altogether, equals, mental calculation, method

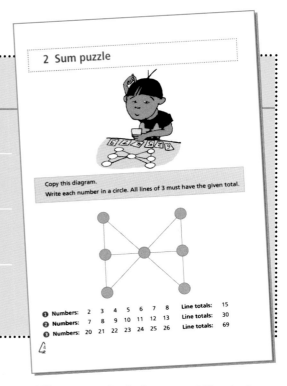

2 Sum puzzle

Copy this diagram.
Write each number in a circle. All lines of 3 must have the given total.

① Numbers: 2   3   4   5   6   7   8   Line totals: 15
② Numbers: 7   8   9 10 11 12 13   Line totals: 30
③ Numbers: 20 21 22 23 24 25 26   Line totals: 69

4

What's the problem?

A puzzle in which children arrange given numbers in a diagram, so that lines of 3 numbers have the same given total. It involves mental addition of 3 numbers. Methods can range from guesswork to systematic reasoning about numbers.

Problem solving objectives

- Explain methods and reasoning about numbers orally and in writing.
- Solve mathematical problems or puzzles, recognise and explain patterns and relationships, generalise and predict. Suggest extensions by asking 'What if . . .?'

Differentiation

All children work from Textbook page 4.

More able: problem 3 (based on numbers 20 to 26).

Average: problem 2 (same problem but based on numbers 7 to 13).

Less able: problem 1 (same problem but based on numbers 2 to 8).

Differentiation will also be through the methods used.

Introducing the problem

Provide addition questions involving 2 and 3 numbers. Include examples for the less able and the more able, e.g. $6 + 7$, $3 + 4 + 5$, $12 + 19$, $24 + 25 + 26$, $38 + 27$, $139 + 29 + 17$. For each one, ask children to calculate the total mentally and to explain how they calculated their answer.

Offer some 'difference' calculations, e.g. *What is the difference between 35 and 16? What must I add to 39 to make 54?*

Read through the instructions for the puzzle on Textbook page 4. Explain that it is possible for the puzzle to be solved through guesswork, but you would like children to think carefully about the puzzle and to try to find a strategy for solving it.

Teacher focus for activity

All children: Children may find it helpful to write their numbers on small pieces of card to move around on their diagram.

Discuss any strategies that children are using. If, after some time, children are still using guesswork, consider asking one or more of the following 'leading' questions to nudge them towards a strategy:

- *Which three of the numbers have a total of 15 (30, 69)?*
- *Do any other sets of three numbers have the same total?*
- *Could you find them all? How could you use this information?*
- *How many sums does the centre circle belong to? (3) . . . and the 'corner' circles? (2) . . . and the 'side' circles? (2)*

Solving the puzzle will involve not only addition but also finding differences, e.g. when 2 numbers have been added, finding what number needs to be added to make the target total. Ask children to explain methods used for adding, finding a difference or finding a set of numbers with the target total.

Optional adult input

Work with the Less able group. Help children to find combinations of three numbers with a total of 15. Play a game with digit cards in which each child has to select a different combination of 3 digits with a total of 15.

Plenary

Copy the diagram from Textbook page 4 on the board, together with each set of numbers and their line total.

1 Ask children from each group to show their solutions and to outline their methods. Elicit that there is more than one correct arrangement for each set of numbers. Together, check that each solution is correct. In the process of checking, take the opportunity to discuss mental strategies for adding each line of numbers.

Congratulate those children who reasoned about numbers or devised a strategy.

2 Go over the following approach to problem 2. Explain that the same procedure can be used with the other puzzles.

Establish that it would be useful to know which sets of 3 numbers have a total of 30.

Discuss systematic ways of finding all the possible combinations with a total of 30. One way would be to start by adding the two smallest numbers, 7 and 8, and finding the number that, when added to the total, gives 30; then repeat for 7 and 9, then 7 and 10 . . .; then repeat starting with 8 and 9, then 8 and 10 . . .

(For the importance of being systematic when finding all possible combinations see **Useful mathematical information**, page 85.)

Invite children to help you compile an ordered list such as this:
7 + 8 + 15
7 + 9 + 14
(discard because 14 and 15 are not given numbers)
7 + 10 + 13
7 + 11 + 12
(establish that the '7' combinations start repeating from here)
8 + 9 + 13
8 + 10 + 12
8 + 11 + 11
(discard because you can only use 11 once)
(establish that the '8' combinations start repeating from here)
9 + 10 + 11
(establish that all combinations start repeating from here)

So the only possible combinations of 3 numbers with a total of 30 are:
7 + 10 + 13; 7 + 11 + 12; 8 + 9 + 13; 8 + 10 + 12;
9 + 10 + 11

Point out that, conveniently, there are five lines of 3 numbers in the diagram and five possible sums.

Ask: *How many sums is the centre number included in?* (3) *So what must the centre number be?*

Establish that as 10 is the only number that appears in three of the sums above, it must be the centre number.

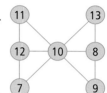

Once this is inserted in the centre circle, the other numbers from the sums that include the 10 can be entered into the diagram, ensuring that the additions 7 + 11 + 12 and 8 + 9 + 13 are represented down the sides of the diagram.

Development

Children investigate the effect on line totals of adding or subtracting 1 or any other constant to or from each given number. Can they use what they find out to create their own puzzles using the same diagram?

Solutions

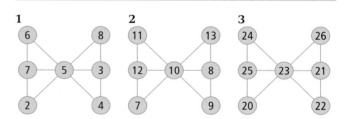

There are other possible arrangements of the numbers around the central number in each diagram.

3 Animal farm

What's the problem?

There are 2 types of farm animal in a field. Children are given the fraction of the total that is one type and the total number of legs in the field. Using their understanding of fractions and reasoning about numbers, children calculate the number of each type of animal.

Problem solving objectives

- Choose and use appropriate number operations and appropriate ways of calculating to solve problems.
- Explain methods and reasoning about numbers orally and in writing.
- Solve mathematical problems or puzzles, recognise and explain patterns and relationships, generalise and predict. Suggest extensions by asking 'What if . . .?'

Differentiation

Children work from different parts of PCM 1.

More able: Animal farm 3.

Average: Animal farm 2 (similar but simpler problem, with a clue).

Less able: Animal farm 1 (similar but even simpler problem, with a clue).

Introducing the problem

Revise fractions of numbers in the context of animals, e.g. *There are horses and sheep in a field. One third of the animals are sheep. If there are 12 animals, how many are sheep? How many are horses? What if there are 15, 18, 21 . . . animals?*

Repeat with other fractions and numbers. Relate the finding of fractions to division.

Explain that this lesson's problems involve fractions. Read through each problem (omitting the clues). Emphasise the importance in problem solving of carefully recording work. (Recording as they work reminds children of what they have done so far, and, when they have finished, enables others to understand how they solved the problem.)

Teacher focus for activity

All children: Encourage children to be systematic when trialling different numbers of animals, and to look for patterns. The 2, 4 and 8 times-tables are involved and opportunities may arise of discussing how facts for one table can be derived from another (see **Useful mathematical information**, pages 85–86).

More able: If children are struggling to get started, ask: *What is the smallest number of animals there could be?* (8) *Why?* (If there was only 1 goat, which is one eighth of the animals, there must be 8 animals altogether.) *So, how many goats and how many chickens is that?* (1 goat and 7 chickens)

Look out for children who think the smallest possible numbers of each are 1 and 8.

How many legs will there be? (18) *What are the next smallest possible numbers? . . .*

Average: Ask similar questions to those suggested for the More able group. Here, the smallest numbers are 1 cow and 2 turkeys (8 legs).

Less able: Encourage children to continue the process suggested in their clue, calculating the number of legs each time.

Optional adult input

Work with the More able group. Discuss their methods of calculating the total number of legs for each trial set of animals.

Plenary

Display a large copy of PCM 1.

1 Invite children from all groups to describe how they solved their problem. Discuss and compare differences in approaches, particularly with regard to how systematic or random they are.

Establish that one systematic method is to investigate numbers of animals and legs starting with the smallest possible number of each type of animal and working upwards.

2 Focus on Animal farm 2.

Draw this table (with just the headings).

animals	cows	turkeys	legs
3	1	2	8
6	2	4	16
9	3	6	24
12	4	8	32
15	5	10	40
18	6	12	48

What is the smallest number of animals there could be? (3) Why?

Establish that as the number of cows is one third of the total, the total must be divisible by 3 (a multiple of 3).

So what are the smallest numbers of cows and turkeys possible?

Establish that one third of 3 is 1 so 1 cow and 2 turkeys (3 − 1) are the smallest numbers possible. Enter this into the table. *How many legs do 1 cow and 2 turkeys have? How did you work it out?*

Consider other numbers of cows and turkeys, discussing methods of calculating the total number of legs each time, e.g. multiplying the number of cows by 4 and the number of turkeys by 2, and adding; multiplying the number of cows by 4 and doubling (since the number of cows' legs and turkeys' legs in each row are the same).

Children should notice the multiples of 8 in the 'legs' column. Ask: *Why multiples of 8?* (1 cow and 2 turkeys have 8 legs altogether.)

Finally establish that for there to be 48 legs altogether, there must be 12 turkeys (and 6 cows). Invite children to check that this result satisfies the conditions of the problem.

3 Briefly deal with Animal farm 1 in a similar way.

animals	sheep	geese	legs
2	1	1	6
4	2	2	12
6	3	3	18
8	4	4	24
10	5	5	30
12	6	6	36
14	7	7	42

- Establish that the total number of animals must be divisible by 2 (a multiple of 2; an even number), if half of the animals are sheep.
- Discuss methods of calculating the number of legs.
- Discuss why the numbers of legs are multiples of 6. (1 sheep and 1 goose have a total of 6 legs)
- Confirm the result for 42 legs as 7 sheep (and 7 geese).

4 Briefly deal with Animal farm 3 in a similar way.

animals	goats	chickens	legs
8	1	7	18
16	2	14	36
24	3	21	54
32	4	28	72
40	5	35	90
48	6	42	108

- Establish that the total number of animals must be divisible by 8 (a multiple of 8), if one eighth of the animals are goats.
- Discuss methods of calculating the number of legs.
- Discuss why the numbers of legs are multiples of 18. (1 goat and 7 chickens have a total of 18 legs)
- Confirm the result for 108 legs as 42 chickens (and 6 goats).

Development

Children investigate ways in which their problem can be modified yet remain solvable, e.g. changing the fraction or changing the number of animals.

Solutions

Animal farm 1: 7 sheep

Animal farm 2: 12 turkeys

Animal farm 3: 42 chickens

4 Money bags

Minimum prior experience

mental addition of single-digit numbers

Resources

Textbook page 5, PCM 2, 1p coins or counters or cubes, bank cash bags (optional)

Key vocabulary

add, total, altogether, equals, relationship, sequence, pattern

4 Money bags

❶ Jenny divided 15 pennies among 4 money bags.
She could then pay any amount from 1p to 15p just by giving bags.
How many pennies did Jenny put in each bag?

❷ Marcus divided 31 pennies among 5 money bags.
He could then pay any amount from 1p to 31p just by giving bags.

a How many pennies did Marcus put in each bag?

b Can you see a relationship between the amounts of money in the bags?
Describe the relationship.

c What if Marcus has one more money bag?
What is the smallest amount he needs to put in it to make any amount from 1p to 63p?

What's the problem?

Children divide a given number of pennies among a given number of money bags. They work out how many pennies need to be put in each bag so that any sum of money, up to a given amount, can be paid just using the unopened bags. The problem involves adding small amounts, reasoning about numbers and possibly the identification of number relationships.

Problem solving objectives

- Explain methods and reasoning about numbers orally and in writing.
- Solve mathematical problems or puzzles, recognise and explain patterns and relationships, generalise and predict. Suggest extensions by asking 'What if . . .?'

Differentiation

More able: Textbook page 5, problem 2.

Average: Textbook page 5, problem 1 (similar problem but with fewer bags and a smaller amount).

Less able: PCM 2 (same problem as Average but with a clue and preceded by a 'warm-up' problem).

Differentiation will also be through the methods used.

Introducing the problem

Talk about small plastic cash bags of the type used by banks. Have children ever seen any? Show some if you have any available. Explain that these are usually for fixed amounts of money that are written on the bag, e.g. '£10 in 2p coins'.

Establish the general problem: a child has a number of pennies and a number of bags; they put a certain amount in each bag so that they can pay any amount (up to a given amount) just by giving bags and without opening them.

Remind children to record their workings.

Teacher focus for activity

All children: Children may find it helpful to manipulate 1p coins, counters or cubes on 'bags' drawn on paper (the Less able group can use cubes on the bags on the PCM).

Initially, children may use a fairly random approach, trying different numbers of pennies in each bag and then checking that each amount can be made. If, after some time, children appear to be making little headway with this approach, encourage a more systematic approach by asking: *What are the minimum amounts you would need in each bag to make 1p?* (1p in one bag) *To make 1p and 2p?* (1p in two of the bags) *To make 1p, 2p and 3p?* (1p in one bag and 2p in another) . . . (Note that problem 2 on PCM 2 stipulates that there must be a different amount in each bag, so 1p in two of the bags is not an option.)

Optional adult input

Work with the Less able group. For problem 2, use drawings of 4 money bags and 15 pennies, counters or cubes, and invite children to put the minimum amount required on each bag to make 1p, 2p, 3p . . . 15p with a different amount in each bag.

Plenary

1 Invite children to give their solutions to each problem and to outline the strategies they used. Discuss the advantages of systematic methods, e.g. they are generally more efficient (quicker and entail less work) and guarantee a result.

2 Focus on problem 1 on Textbook page 5. Establish that this is essentially the same as problem 2 on PCM 2. **Draw 4 money bags.**

Consider a total of 1p. Establish that one of the bags must contain 1 penny. Draw a penny in one of the bags.

Consider 2p. *What must we have in one of the other bags so that 2p can be paid?*

Establish that a bag containing either 1 penny or 2 pennies is required. Debate which would be preferable. Conclude that a bag containing 2 pennies would be preferable as, with the original 1 penny bag, 1p, 2p and 3p can now be paid. Draw 2 pennies in the second bag.

Consider 4p. *What must one of the remaining bags contain so that 4p can be paid?*

Discuss the various options: 1, 2, 3 and 4 pennies, e.g. 1 penny in the bag, together with the other two bags, enables just 1p, 2p, 3p and 4p to be paid; 2 pennies in the bag, together with the others, enables amounts up to 5p to be paid; 3 pennies in the bag enables all amounts up to 6p to be paid. However, putting 4 pennies in the bag is preferable as it enables amounts up to 7p to be paid. Invite children to demonstrate how. Draw 4 pennies in the third bag.

  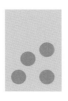

Ask: *So what amount will we need in the last bag?* Establish that as the problem stipulates 15 pennies

and that 7 pennies have been used, then the fourth bag must contain 15 − 7 = 8 pennies. Draw 8 pennies in the fourth bag.

Invite children to check that all amounts up to 15p can be paid.

3 Invite children to describe any relationship they can see between the four amounts. They may notice that the amount in each bag is double the amount in the preceding bag. *If there were 5 bags, what do you think the fifth bag would contain?* (16p)

Ask children from the More able group to confirm that 16p in the fifth bag is a correct prediction.

(See **Useful mathematical information**, page 86 for the connection between these problems and the binary numeration system.)

Development

Children show how amounts up to 63p can be made using bags containing 1p, 2p, 4p, 8p, 16p and 32p using the fewest bags possible each time.

Solutions

Textbook page 4

1 1p, 2p, 4p, 8p

2 a 1p, 2p, 4p, 8p, 16p
   b When the amounts in each bag are ordered (smallest first), each amount is double the preceding amount.
   c 32p

PCM 2

1 1p, 2p, 4p

2 1p, 2p, 4p, 8p

5 Computer crash!

Minimum prior experience

mental addition and subtraction of numbers to 10

Resources

Textbook pages 6 and 7, counters or cubes

Key vocabulary

score, sum, total, add, plus, altogether, increase, decrease, method

What's the problem?

Given the sums of pairs of scores for a computer game and the total of all scores, children work out the individual scores. The problem involves trial and improvement methods, reasoning about numbers and the mental addition and subtraction of up to five 1- and 2-digit numbers.

Problem solving objectives

- Explain methods and reasoning about numbers orally and in writing.
- Solve mathematical problems or puzzles, recognise and explain patterns and relationships, generalise and predict. Suggest extensions by asking 'What if . . .?'

Differentiation

More able: Textbook page 7, problem 3 (involving adding numbers to 50).

Average: Textbook page 7, problem 2 (similar problem but with numbers from 10 to 20).

Less able: Textbook page 6, problem 1 (similar problem but with numbers to 10).

Introducing the problem

Give children pairs of numbers to add mentally, e.g. 48 + 59, 25 + 26, 32 + 75, 17 + 37. Each time, discuss different methods of mental calculation that children used. Explain that the problems today involve the addition of 2 or more numbers.

Set the context of the problems. Discuss children's experiences of computer 'crashes'. Have they lost

valuable work as a result? Have they been able to retrieve the work?

Let children read through the problem and make sure they understand what is required before they start.

Teacher focus for activity

All children: The likely initial strategy will be: choose one possible pair of scores for, say, Ann and Ben; use Ben's possible score to determine Ceri's; determine Dave's, then Elvis's, scores; find the total of all the scores to check whether it tallies with the given total.

At this stage, if the two totals do not tally, encourage children to reason about what pair of scores for Ann and Ben to try next. Encourage them to think about the effect on the final total of increasing/decreasing Ann's score by 1, 2, 3, . . . (increase/decrease the total by 1, 2, 3, . . .)

Help children to devise a clear recording system. (The children's names can be abbreviated to A, B, C, D and E.)

When children are adding numbers, discuss their mental methods.

Optional adult input

Work with the Less able group helping them to reason. Ask: *What could Ann and Ben's scores be?* (0 and 6, 1 and 5, 2 and 4, 3 and 3, 4 and 2, 5 and 1 or 6 and 0) *What shall we try first? So what will the other scores be? What is the total? So, are the scores correct? What shall we try next? . . .*

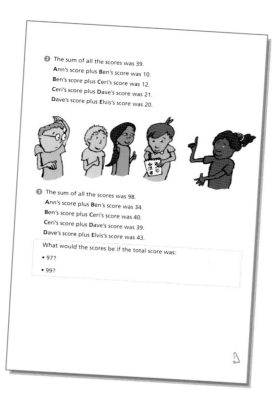

② The sum of all the scores was 39.
Ann's score plus Ben's score was 10.
Ben's score plus Ceri's score was 12.
Ceri's score plus Dave's score was 21.
Dave's score plus Elvis's score was 20.

③ The sum of all the scores was 98.
Ann's score plus Ben's score was 34.
Ben's score plus Ceri's score was 40.
Ceri's score plus Dave's score was 39.
Dave's score plus Elvis's score was 43.

What would the scores be if the total score was:
• 97?
• 99?

Plenary

1 Explain that together, you are going to solve a similar problem to theirs, but using different numbers. The same methods they have been using can be used here.

Write these pairs of scores and the total of the individual scores:

Ann and Ben	**31**
Ben and Ceri	**35**
Ceri and Dave	**36**
Dave and Elvis	**28**
Total score	**76**

Discuss ways to represent the data. Choose one of the children's ways or use this format (letters are initial letters of names):

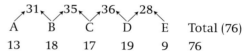

$$\overset{31}{\underset{A \quad B}{\diagdown}} \overset{35}{\underset{B \quad C}{\diagup\diagdown}} \overset{36}{\underset{C \quad D}{\diagup\diagdown}} \overset{28}{\underset{D \quad E}{\diagup\diagdown}} \qquad \text{Total (76)}$$

2 *How could we start?* A likely suggestion is that a pair of scores totalling 31 is tried for Ann and Ben, and the other scores calculated accordingly. Establish that, alternatively, scores could be tried for other pairs of children.

What scores for Ann and Ben could we try first? Discuss responses. Any pair of numbers totalling 31 would be appropriate. Establish that 0 and 31 would be a logical pair to start with, but are unlikely scores.

Here we will try 15 and 16, but the overall procedure will be similar whatever pair is chosen.

Enter 15 and 16 under the appropriate letters:

A	B	C	D	E	Total (76)
15	**16**	19	17	11	78

(with the 31, 35, 36, 28 diagram above: A–B 31, B–C 35, C–D 36, D–E 28)

Invite children to calculate other scores and explain their methods of calculation, e.g. to find Ceri's score, the difference between 16 and 35 must be found. This could be done by counting on 4 to reach 20 and then adding another 15 to reach 35. So Ceri's score is 4 + 15 = 19

Finally, the five scores need to be added to find the total. Again, discuss methods of calculation, e.g. 15 + 16 + 19 + 17 + 11 could be regarded as four 15s with adjustments made before finally adding the 11:

$$(4 \times 15) + 1 + 4 + 2 + 11 = 60 + 18 = 78$$

Establish that the score is 78 and that this is 2 more than the given total.

3 Discuss which scores for Ann and Ben could be tried next, asking children to justify their choices based on their own investigations. Establish that decreasing Ann's score by 2 and adjusting the other scores accordingly produces a total score of 76.

A	B	C	D	E	Total (76)
13	18	17	19	9	76

(with the 31, 35, 36, 28 diagram above: A–B 31, B–C 35, C–D 36, D–E 28)

Confirm that the children's scores are as follows:

Ann 13, Ben 18, Ceri 17, Dave 19, Elvis 9

Development

Children make up similar problems for each other to solve. Encourage them to change the context. They will also need to ensure that the problem 'works'.

Solutions

1 Ann 2, Ben 4, Ceri 6, Dave 1, Elvis 8

2 Ann 7, Ben 3, Ceri 9, Dave 12, Elvis 8

3 Ann 15, Ben 19, Ceri 21, Dave 18, Elvis 25

Total 97: Ann 14, Ben 20, Ceri 20, Dave 19, Elvis 24
Total 99: Ann 16, Ben 18, Ceri 22, Dave 17, Elvis 26

6 Sponsored walk

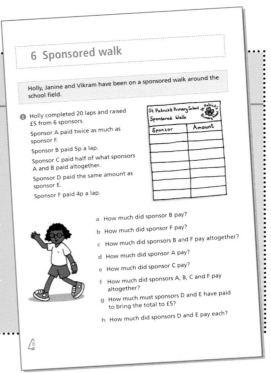

Minimum prior experience

multiplication by 2, 4 and 5; addition of money; halving amounts of money

Resources

Textbook pages 8 and 9

Key vocabulary

amount, half, twice as much, altogether, total, add, multiply, data

What's the problem?

A 'real-life' money problem in the context of a sponsored walk. Children reason about given data to find unknown data, choosing appropriate number operations and methods of calculation, including addition of two or more amounts, multiplication, and halving amounts of money.

Problem solving objectives

- Choose and use appropriate number operations and appropriate ways of calculating to solve problems.
- Explain methods and reasoning about numbers orally and in writing.
- Use all four operations to solve word problems involving numbers in 'real life', and money, using one or more steps, including converting pounds to pence.

Differentiation

More able: Textbook page 9, problem 3.

Average: Textbook page 9, problem 2 (smaller numbers and easier calculations).

Less able: Textbook page 8, problem 1 (even smaller numbers and easier calculations, and step-by-step presentation).

Introducing the problem

Discuss sponsored events children have been involved in. What were they raising money for? How much money did they raise? How many sponsors did they get? How did the sponsorship work? . . .

Explain that the problems are about a sponsored walk. Give children a few minutes to read through their problem and answer any queries.

Remind them to record all their working.

Teacher focus for activity

All children: Children may find it helpful to list A, B, C, D, E and F and write the amounts by the side as they are found.

More able and Average: Discuss problem solving strategies that children are using and their methods of calculation. Encourage mental methods whenever possible.

For children who appear to be making no headway, ask one or more of the following 'leading' questions:

- *Which amounts could we work out straight away?* (B and F)
- *What amount could we work out now?* (A, as it's twice F)
- *Knowing the amounts for A and B what could we work out next?* (C, as it's half the total of A and B)
- *Knowing the amounts for A, B, C and F, what could we work out now?* (the total for D and E, then D and E individually)

Encourage children who have found the solution to devise a checking strategy, e.g. by adding all the separate sponsorship amounts to see if the total tallies with the given total.

Less able: The problem solving strategy is more or less laid out. However, you may need to discuss methods of calculation with children.

2 Janine completed 34 laps and raised £11.63 from 6 sponsors.

Sponsor A paid twice as much as sponsor F.
Sponsor B paid 5p a lap.
Sponsor C paid half of what sponsors A and B paid altogether.
Sponsor D paid the same amount as sponsor E.
Sponsor F paid 4p a lap.

How much did sponsor E pay?

3 Vikram completed 69 laps and raised £31.38 from 6 sponsors.

Sponsor A paid twice as much as sponsor F.
Sponsor B paid 8p a lap.
Sponsor C paid half of what sponsors A and B paid altogether.
Sponsor D paid the same amount as sponsor E.
Sponsor F paid 6p a lap.

How much did sponsor E pay?

Optional adult input

Work with the Average group, helping children to deduce an appropriate order in which to use the information, and discussing methods of calculation.

Plenary

1 Focus on problem 2. Explain that all problems are similar (but with different numbers and amounts) so problem solving methods will be exactly the same. Read through the problem and discuss the order in which the clues can be used.

2 Work through the problem together. At each step discuss the calculations involved and methods of calculation that could be used. Steps are likely to be as follows:

Calculate the amount for:
1 sponsor B (5p × 34 = 170p = £1.70);
2 sponsor F (4p × 34 = 136p = £1.36);
3 sponsor A (£1.36 × 2 = £2.72);
4 sponsors A and B (£2.72 + £1.70 = £4.42);
5 sponsor C ($\frac{1}{2}$ of £4.42 = £2.21);
6 sponsors A, B, C and F altogether
   (£2.72 + £1.70 + £2.21 + £1.36 = £7.99);
7 sponsors D and E (subtracting amounts for sponsors A, B, C and F from the total sponsorship amount: £11.63 − £7.99 = £3.64);
8 sponsor E (dividing the total for sponsors D and E by 2: £3.64 ÷ 2 = £1.82)

Here are some suggestions for methods of calculation that could be included in the discussions:

- **Steps 1 and 2 (4p × 34 and 5p × 34)**

  Children should be aware that multiplication is commutative, i.e. the numbers can be reversed without affecting the answer, e.g. 4 × 34 = 34 × 4. In other words, 34 lots of 4p is equivalent to 4 lots of 34p. (For more about the associative, commutative and distributive laws see **Useful mathematical information**, pages 86–87.)

  4 × 34 could be calculated by doubling 34 (68) and doubling again (136). (See **Useful mathematical information**, page 85 on the relationship between the 2 and 4 times-tables.)

  5 × 34 could be calculated by multiplying 34 by 10 (340) and halving (170).

  Ensure children understand how to convert the results (in pence) to pounds.

- **Step 3 (£1.36 × 2)**

  The pounds and pence components could be calculated separately and the results combined: £1 × 2 = £2; 36p × 2 = 72p; £2 + 72p = £2.72

- **Step 6 (£2.72 + £1.70 + £2.21 + £1.36)**

  This could be done mentally and with jottings in three stages, by adding pairs of amounts and adding the results, e.g.

  - £1.70 + £1.36 = £3.06
    (making use of the fact that 70p and 30p = £1)

  - £2.72 + £2.21 = £4.93
    (no 'carrying' involved here)

  - £3.06 + £4.93 = £7.99
    (again, no carrying involved)

- **Step 7 (£11.63 − £7.99)**

  One method would be to subtract £8 from £11.63 (£3.63) and adjust by adding 1p (£3.64).

Development

Children change amounts, numbers and fractions in the problem to create new problems for each other. They must check that their new problem is solvable.

Solutions

1 a £1.00
   b £0.80 (or 80p)
   c £1.80
   d £1.60
   e £1.30
   f £4.70
   g £0.30 (or 30p)
   h £0.15 (or 15p)

2 £1.82

3 £3.27

7 Shape mobiles

Minimum prior experience

recognition of triangles and squares; multiplication and division by 3 and 4, or ability to generate multiples of 3 and 4; simple mental addition

Resources

Textbook page 10, straws or matchsticks, a 'skeletal' polygon made from straws

Key vocabulary

triangle, square, pentagon, hexagon, octagon, multiple of, divisible by, subtract, times, multiply, divide

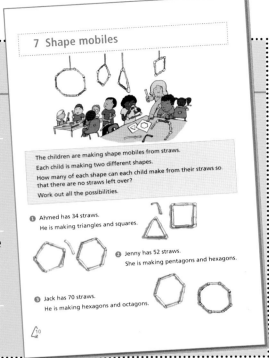

The children are making shape mobiles from straws.
Each child is making two different shapes.
How many of each shape can each child make from their straws so that there are no straws left over?
Work out all the possibilities.

❶ Ahmed has 34 straws.
He is making triangles and squares.

❷ Jenny has 52 straws.
She is making pentagons and hexagons.

❸ Jack has 70 straws.
He is making hexagons and octagons.

What's the problem?

Children investigate the number of each of two shapes that can be made from a given number of straws without any left over. The problem involves the generation of multiples, mental calculations, properties of numbers, patterns and, ideally, an ability to work systematically.

Problem solving objectives

- Choose and use appropriate number operations and appropriate ways of calculating to solve problems.
- Explain methods and reasoning about numbers orally and in writing.
- Solve mathematical problems or puzzles, recognise and explain patterns and relationships, generalise and predict.

Differentiation

All children work from Textbook page 10.

More able: problem 3 (hexagons and octagons; 70 straws).

Average: problem 2 (pentagons and hexagons; 52 straws).

Less able: problem 1 (triangles and squares; 34 straws).

Introducing the problem

Explain that the problems are about making shapes, by joining straws, to hang up as mobiles. Show an example.

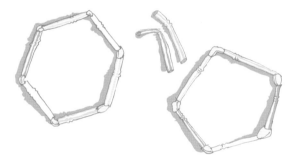

Revise definitions of triangles, squares, pentagons, hexagons and octagons. Ask children to calculate the total number of straws that would be needed for various numbers of shapes, e.g. 6 triangles (18), 4 octagons (32), 5 pentagons (25). Then ask them to calculate the total number of straws needed for combinations of shapes, e.g. 4 triangles and 2 hexagons (24); 4 pentagons and 3 octagons (44).

Read through the problems. Remind children that they should record their work carefully for use in the plenary.

Teacher focus for activity

All children: Initially, children may work fairly randomly, e.g. with problem 2, trying 3 pentagons (15 straws), then seeing if the remaining straws (52 − 15 = 37) can be used up with hexagons (6 won't go into 37, so, no). If they continue to work in this way, encourage them to think of a more systematic way of working.

Encourage children who do not know a particular times-table or set of multiples, to derive them from a known times-table or set of multiples, e.g. the 4, 6 or

8 times-tables can be derived by doubling answers in the 2, 3 and 4 times-tables, respectively (see **Useful mathematical information**, pages 85–86).

Less able: Children may find it helpful to use 34 straws, or matchsticks. If children use straws to actually make the shapes, ask: *Is there a quicker way of using the straws, than making the shapes?* (e.g. bundling them in 3s and 4s to represent the triangles and squares that can be made)

Optional adult input

Work with the Less able group. Help children to reason and work systematically:

If you made 1 square, how many straws would be left? Could you make an exact number of triangles with them? If you made 2 squares, how many straws would be left? . . .

Plenary

1 Explain that you are going to focus on problem 2, but that the same strategies can be used for all of problems.

Read through problem 2. Ask children to explain how they would tackle the problem, based on their own investigation. Discuss each approach. Congratulate children who suggest systematic approaches.

2 Go over the following likely approach:

Consider 1, 2, 3, 4, 5 . . . hexagons, ascertaining each time whether the remaining number of straws is divisible by 5.

Draw this table on the board, and ask children to help you complete it.

hexagons	straws used	straws remaining	divisible by 5?	pentagons
1	$1 \times 6 = 6$	$52 - 6 = 46$	no	
2	$2 \times 6 = 12$	$52 - 12 = 40$	yes	$40 \div 5 = 8$
3	$3 \times 6 = 18$	$52 - 18 = 34$	no	
4	$4 \times 6 = 24$	$52 - 24 = 28$	no	
5	$5 \times 6 = 30$	$52 - 30 = 22$	no	
6	$6 \times 6 = 36$	$52 - 36 = 16$	no	
7	$7 \times 6 = 42$	$52 - 42 = 10$	yes	$10 \div 5 = 2$
8	$8 \times 6 = 48$	$52 - 48 = 4$	no	

For children who do not know the 6 times-table, show them how it can be derived by doubling the 3 times-table (see **Useful mathematical information**, pages 85–86). Discuss children's mental methods of subtraction for the 'straws remaining' column. Discuss also how numbers that are divisible by 5 (multiples of 5) can be recognised (they end with 0 or 5).

Establish that it is not necessary to consider more than 8 hexagons, as these alone would use more than the 52 straws. Establish that 2 hexagons and 8 pentagons or 7 hexagons and 2 pentagons will use exactly 52 straws.

Establish that alternatively 1, 2, 3, 4 . . . pentagons can be considered, ascertaining each time whether hexagons can be made from the remaining straws. If there is time, it would be worthwhile doing this to show that the results are exactly the same.

pentagons	straws used	straws remaining	divisible by 6?	hexagons
1	$1 \times 5 = 5$	$52 - 5 = 47$	no	
2	$2 \times 5 = 10$	$52 - 10 = 42$	yes	$42 \div 6 = 7$
3	$3 \times 5 = 15$	$52 - 15 = 37$	no	
4	$4 \times 5 = 20$	$52 - 20 = 32$	no	
5	$5 \times 5 = 25$	$52 - 25 = 27$	no	
6	$6 \times 5 = 30$	$52 - 30 = 22$	no	
7	$7 \times 5 = 35$	$52 - 35 = 17$	no	
8	$8 \times 5 = 40$	$52 - 40 = 12$	yes	$12 \div 6 = 2$
9	$9 \times 5 = 45$	$52 - 45 = 7$	no	
10	$10 \times 5 = 50$	$52 - 50 = 2$	no	

An alternative solution, which you may wish to introduce, is shown in **Useful mathematical information**, page 87.

Development

With the same number of straws as for their initial investigation, children investigate in a similar way:

More able: heptagons and octagons.

Average: pentagons and heptagons.

Less able: triangles and pentagons.

Solutions

1 2 triangles and 7 squares;
 6 triangles and 4 squares;
 10 triangles and 1 square.

2 2 pentagons and 7 hexagons;
 8 pentagons and 2 hexagons.

3 1 hexagon and 8 octagons;
 5 hexagons and 5 octagons;
 9 hexagons and 2 octagons.

8 Number line race

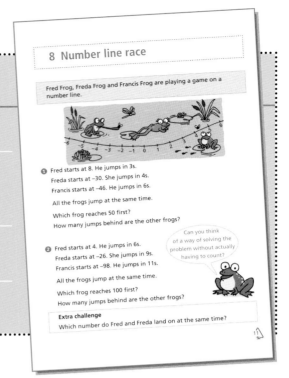

8 Number line race

Fred Frog, Freda Frog and Francis Frog are playing a game on a number line.

❶ Fred starts at 8. He jumps in 3s.
Freda starts at –30. She jumps in 4s.
Francis starts at –46. He jumps in 6s.
All the frogs jump at the same time.
Which frog reaches 50 first?
How many jumps behind are the other frogs?

❷ Fred starts at 4. He jumps in 6s.
Freda starts at –26. She jumps in 9s.
Francis starts at –98. He jumps in 11s.
All the frogs jump at the same time.
Which frog reaches 100 first?
How many jumps behind are the other frogs?

Can you think of a way of solving the problem without actually having to count?

Extra challenge
Which number do Fred and Freda land on at the same time?

Minimum prior experience

counting forwards and backwards, in steps of 2, 3 or 4, from any number (including negative numbers) on a number line

Resources

Textbook page 11, PCM 3, blank number lines

Key vocabulary

positive, negative, above/below zero, sequence, pattern, continue, number line

What's the problem?

Investigating sequences generated by counting on in equal steps along a number line, to find out which sequence generates a given number first. The investigation could involve calculating the difference between a negative and a positive number and dividing the difference.

Problem solving objectives

- Choose and use appropriate number operations and appropriate ways of calculating to solve problems.
- Explain methods and reasoning about numbers orally and in writing.
- Solve mathematical problems or puzzles, recognise and explain patterns and relationships, generalise and predict.

Differentiation

More able: Textbook page 11, problem 2 (range: –100 to 100; steps of 6, 9 and 11). There is also an extra challenge.

Average: Textbook page 11, problem 1 (range: –50 to 50; steps of 3, 4 and 6).

Less able: PCM 3 (range: –20 to 25; steps of 2, 3 and 4).

Differentiation will also be through methods used.

Introducing the problem

Draw a –10 to 10 number line. Invite children to count along it forwards and backwards in various constant steps, e.g.

- start at –1 and count forwards in 2s (–1, 1, 3, 5, 7, 9);
- start at 7 and count backwards in 3s (7, 4, 1, –2, –5, –8).

Repeat, with the whole class saying the numbers up to, say, 50 or –50.

Explain that the problems are about counting along a number line, but that it is actually possible to solve them without having to do any counting. Give children a few minutes to read through their problem and to ask any questions before they start.

Teacher focus for activity

All children: The majority of children will solve the problem by counting in the various steps and recording the numbers. As they do this, encourage them to identify and explain patterns that will assist them, e.g. with problem 2 on Textbook page 11, when counting in 9s from 19 to 91, the units digit decreases by 1 each time while the tens digit increases by 1. *Why is this?* (adding 9 is equivalent to adding 10 and subtracting 1)

You may need to point out that the number **after** the starting number is the result of the first jump – not the starting number itself.

More able and Average: Encourage children to record their work systematically. For each number in a sequence, they will need to know which jump number it was a result of. You could suggest that they devise a table of some sort to keep recordings manageable.

More able: Ask: *Is it possible to work out how many steps it takes to get from each start number to 100 without actually counting?*

Optional adult input

Work with the Average group. Discuss ways of recording jumps (e.g. on a number line or in a table).

Plenary

1 Ask children from each group to give their solutions and to describe their approach. Establish that one method of solving the problem is to work out the numbers that each frog landed on for each jump.

2 Discuss the ways in which children recorded the numbers. Establish that numbers need to be recorded carefully and that a table is an appropriate format. Draw a table similar to the one on PCM 3 as an example, or use one of the children's suggestions.

3 Read through PCM 3, establishing the starting numbers and jump size for each frog. Invite children to complete each row of the table:

		jump														
	start	1	2	3	4	5	6	7	8	9	10	11	12	13	14	15
Fred	1	3	5	7	9	11	13	15	17	19	21	23	25				
Freda	−19	−15	−11	−7	−3	1	5	9	13	17	21	25					
Francis	−20	−17	−14	−11	−8	−5	−2	1	4	7	10	13	16	19	22	25	

Discuss how, when counting on in negative integers, the numerical parts of the integers decrease in size. Ask children to identify any patterns they see, e.g. the odd numbers in Fred's row.

Establish that Freda reaches 25 first in 11 jumps; Fred is 1 jump behind; Francis is 4 jumps behind.

4 Deal with the Textbook problems in a similar way, generating similar tables (see **Useful mathematical information**, page 88) and the solutions:

- **Problem 1**

  Fred reaches 50 first in 14 jumps. Freda and Francis are 6 jumps and 2 jumps behind him, respectively.

- **Problem 2**

  Freda reaches 100 first in 14 jumps. Fred and Francis are 2 jumps and 4 jumps behind her, respectively.

An alternative method which the More able group may have suggested, or which you could introduce to them, is suggested in **Useful mathematical information**, pages 88–89.

Development

Children invent similar jumping frog problems for each other to solve, initially involving just 2 frogs.

Solutions

Textbook page 11

1 Fred reaches 50 first (14 jumps).
   Freda is 6 jumps behind (20 jumps).
   Francis is 2 jumps behind (16 jumps).

2 Freda arrives at 100 first (14 jumps).
   Fred is 2 jumps behind (16 jumps).
   Francis is 4 jumps behind (18 jumps).

Extra challenge: 64

PCM 3

Freda reaches 25 first (11 jumps).
Fred is 1 jump behind (12 jumps).
Francis is 4 jumps behind (15 jumps).

9 Fair shares

Minimum prior experience

finding halves of numbers; adding 2

Resources

Textbook page 12, PCM 4, enlarged copy of PCM 4 (optional), counters

Key vocabulary

half, quarter, third, two thirds, increase, decrease, divisible by, multiple of

What's the problem?

An unknown number of sweets is distributed between two children in a given proportion. One child gives a specified number of sweets to the other, so that they have an equal number. Children are asked to work out the original numbers of sweets. The problem involves an understanding of fractions, multiples and divisibility, and an ability to work systematically.

Problem solving objectives

- Explain methods and reasoning about numbers orally and in writing.
- Solve mathematical problems or puzzles, recognise and explain patterns and relationships, generalise and predict.

Differentiation

More able: PCM 4, Fair shares 2.

Average: PCM 4, Fair shares 1 (similar but easier problem; discretionary clue in **Teacher focus for activity**).

Less able: Textbook page 12 (similar but easier problem; clue given).

Differentiation will also be through methods used.

Introducing the problem

Revise finding unit fractions of numbers by asking children to find, e.g. $\frac{1}{2}$ of 20 (10); $\frac{1}{3}$ of 12 (4); $\frac{1}{5}$ of 25 (5); $\frac{1}{6}$ of 36 (6). Relate the finding of fractions to division, e.g. $\frac{1}{3}$ of 9 is found by splitting 9 into 3 equal groups which can be done by dividing 9 by 3.

Read through each problem (but not the clues) and answer any queries children may have. Encourage children to discuss strategies with each other before they start, and to record their work carefully and systematically.

Teacher focus for activity

All children: Discuss the possible numbers of sweets for Amy. (They are all multiples of 3 (More able), 4 (Average) or 2 (Less able), because the required fractions of these multiples result in whole numbers of sweets for Ben; they must be greater than, or equal to, the number of sweets that Amy gives to Ben.)

Discuss the possible numbers of sweets for Ben (any whole number for Average and Less able; any even number for More able).

Encourage children who are already trialling different numbers for Amy or Ben, to do so systematically: trying the smallest possible number first, then the next smallest . . . and looking for patterns as they do so.

Encourage children to record their trials in an orderly way, perhaps as a table.

More able: Help children to understand that, e.g. if **one** third of a number is 4, then **two** thirds of the number is $2 \times 4 = 8$. (For more about finding non-unit fractions of numbers see **Useful mathematical information**, page 89.)

Average: (Discretionary clue for those who are making no headway) *Try different numbers of sweets for Amy.*

Less able: Help children to record their trials in a systematic way. Children may find it helpful to model each trial using counters in two circles, representing Amy and Ben's sweets.

Amy   Ben

Optional adult input

Work with the More able group. Ask children to explain the problem solving strategy they are using and how they will arrive at the answer.

Plenary

Ensure that all children have access to all the problems, e.g. by displaying an enlarged copy of PCM 4 and writing the Textbook problem on the board.

1 Invite children from each group to outline the strategy they used in solving their problem and to give their solution. The most likely method is to trial different numbers for Amy or Ben. Discuss the different ways in which children recorded the trials. Congratulate children who investigated and recorded in a systematic way and who reasoned, e.g. that Amy's number of sweets must be a multiple of 3.

2 Focus on PCM 4, Fair shares 1, encouraging all children to contribute. You could relate some of the suggested questions and discussions to the other problems.

   What is the smallest number of sweets that Amy could have? Establish that if Ben has one quarter of the number of sweets that Amy has, then Amy must have a number divisible by 4 (a multiple of 4). But, in order for Amy to be able to give Ben 12 sweets, she must start with at least 12 sweets. As 12 is a multiple of 4, it is the smallest possibility.

3 **Draw this table and write in the headings** (or use another format suggested by children).

starting numbers		finishing numbers	
Amy	**Ben**	**Amy (− 12)**	**Ben (+ 12)**
12	3	0	15
16	4	4	16
20	5	8	17
24	6	12	18
28	7	16	19
32	8	20	20

   Enter 12 and 3 as starting numbers (although you could debate with the children whether this is worthwhile, as it is obvious that giving Ben 12 sweets would leave Amy with none). Invite children

to calculate the numbers of sweets each would have after Amy has given Ben 12. Enter the results.

Ask children to give you successive possible starting numbers for Amy and Ben, calculating the finishing numbers each time and recording the results. After the first few rows of the table have been completed, invite children to identify patterns and to use these to predict results, e.g. multiples of 4 in Amy's finishing numbers; counting numbers in Ben's columns.

Establish that the sum of each pair of starting numbers and the sum of the matching pair of finishing numbers should be the same (since the total number of sweets is constant). This could be used to check the calculations.

4 Finally establish that both children have equal finishing numbers of sweets when the starting numbers are 32 and 8 for Amy and Ben respectively.

   Is this the only possible solution? If we carried on completing the table, could there be another pair of equal finishing numbers? Discuss children's responses. Establish that the patterns indicate that Amy's finishing numbers are increasing by 4 each time, whereas Ben's are increasing by only 1 each time, so they will not be equal again.

   (For solution tables for the other two problems, see **Useful mathematical information**, page 89.)

Development

What if Ben's fraction was:
Less able: $\frac{1}{3}$?　　**Average:** $\frac{1}{5}$?　　**More able:** $\frac{3}{4}$?

Solutions

PCM 4
Fair shares 1
Amy: 32 sweets　　　　Ben: 8 sweets

Fair shares 2
Amy: 36 sweets　　　　Ben: 24 sweets

Textbook page 12
Amy: 8 sweets　　　　Ben: 4 sweets

10 Puzzling symbols

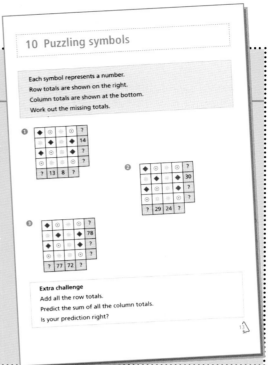

Minimum prior experience

adding several single-digit numbers; subtracting numbers under 20; dividing single-digit numbers by 2 or 4; understanding the relationships between number operations

Resources

Textbook page 13, PCM 5 (with puzzle grids and clues separated), squared paper, three enlarged puzzle grids from PCM 5

Key vocabulary

add, sum, total, subtract, difference, divide, row, column, symbol, represent

What's the problem?

A grid contains symbols representing numbers. The totals of some of the rows and columns are given and children are asked to find the total of the others. This involves the addition of several numbers, subtraction, division and an understanding of the relationships between operations.

Problem solving objectives

- Choose and use appropriate number operations and appropriate ways of calculating to solve problems.
- Explain methods and reasoning about numbers orally and in writing.
- Solve mathematical problems or puzzles, recognise and explain patterns and relationships, generalise and predict.

Differentiation

All children work from Textbook page 13.

More able: problem 3.

Average: problem 2 (same puzzle, smaller numbers).

Less able: problem 1 (same puzzle, even smaller numbers).

Discretionary clues are provided as a cut-off slip on PCM 5.

The extra challenge in the Textbook is suitable for all the problems.

Introducing the problem

Read through the instructions at the top of Textbook page 13. Make sure that children understand the meaning of 'row' and 'column' and that they know that the column and row totals are in the coloured squares. Ensure children understand that they need to work out what column and row totals the question marks represent. Point out the availability of puzzle grids (from PCM 5) or squared paper for recording on.

Teacher focus for activity

All children: If after some time children are making no headway, direct their attention to the column of stars or provide them with the discretionary clues from PCM 5. As children work, ask them which row or column they will work on next and why. (It is only lines with one unknown symbol, and where the total is known, that will be fruitful.)

Calculations will involve addition, subtraction and division. Encourage children to carry them out mentally. Ask them to explain the methods they used.

When children have found the numbers the symbols represent and the totals, ask them how they can check whether their answers are correct. Ask: *What if you added together all the column totals and then added together all the row totals, what would you expect to notice about the answers?* (They should be the same.) *Why?* (Each answer represents the sum of all the symbols in the grid.)

Optional adult input

Work with the Less able group. Help children to reason about the symbols by asking questions, e.g. with the second row down: *What is the row total? What is the sum of the stars? So how many more do you need to make the row total? So what is the total of the diamonds? So what is each diamond?*

Plenary

Display three enlarged puzzle grids from PCM 5 with the given row totals for each problem written in.

Clarify that the layout of the symbols in each grid is the same, so the same steps can be taken to solve each problem. Discuss children's puzzle solving strategies one step at a time. For each step, discuss the calculations involved for each puzzle and calculation strategies, encouraging mental methods. As the values of each symbol are found, write them over the symbol in the displayed puzzles. Here is the most likely sequence of steps, together with the calculations involved for problem 2 (see **Useful mathematical information**, page 90 for solution grids and calculations for problems 1 and 3):

- **Step 1: 3rd column**

  Find the value of the ✱ by dividing the column total by 4.

  $24 \div 4 = 6$

  So, ✱ = 6

- **Step 2: 2nd row**

  Subtract the sum of the two ✱ values from the total to give the sum of the two ◆s. Dividing the sum of the ◆s by 2 will give the value of one ◆.

  $30 - (6 + 6) = 30 - 12 = 18$

  $18 \div 2 = 9$

  So, ◆ = 9

- **Step 3: 2nd column**

  Subtract the values of the ◆ and ✱ from the column total to give the sum of the two ⊙s.

  Divide the sum of the two ⊙s by 2 to give the value of one ⊙.

  $29 - (9 + 6) = 29 - 15 = 14$

  $14 \div 2 = 7$

  So, ⊙ = 7

- **Step 4**

  Find all the missing totals by adding numbers in rows and columns.

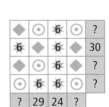

Development

Children make up similar grid puzzles of their own for each other to solve. They must ensure that their puzzle is solvable.

Solutions

1 Rows: 13, (14), 15, 10
  Columns: 15, (13), (8), 16

  Extra challenge: Sum of row and column totals = 52

2 Rows: 29, (30), 31, 26
  Columns: 31, (29), (24), 32

  Extra challenge: Sum of row and column totals = 116

3 Rows: 77, (78), 79, 74
  Columns: 79, (77), (72), 80

  Extra challenge: Sum of row and column totals = 308

11 Seating arrangements

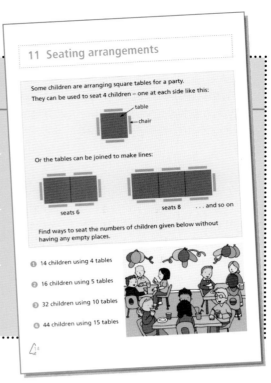

Minimum prior experience

mentally adding numbers to 20

Resources

Textbook page 14, small square tiles, scrap paper

Key vocabulary

even numbers, sequence, add, multiples, divisible by, equal groups of, single, double, triple, increase, decrease

What's the problem?

Children arrange a given number of tables to seat a given number of children, so there are no empty places. Potentially the problem involves trial and improvement methods, systematic working, reasoning about numbers, calculating mentally using one or more of the four operations, and recognition and generation of multiples.

Problem solving objectives

- Choose and use appropriate number operations and appropriate ways of calculating to solve problems.
- Explain methods and reasoning about numbers orally and in writing.
- Solve mathematical problems or puzzles, recognise and explain patterns and relationships, generalise and predict.

Differentiation

All children work from Textbook page 14.

More able: problem 4.

Average: problem 3 (similar problem but with smaller numbers).

Less able: problems 1 and 2 (similar problems but with even smaller numbers).

Differentiation will also be by methods used.

Introducing the problem

Discuss your classroom seating arrangements, e.g. *How many children can be seated around a single table? How many can be seated around 2 (3, 4 . . .) tables pushed together? If there was unlimited space, what would be the maximum number of children that all the tables in the class could accommodate? . . .*

Together look at the problem introduction on Textbook page 14. Ensure children understand that tables can be arranged only in rows of single tables. Remind children to record how they solve their problem and tell them that there may be more than one solution to each problem.

Teacher focus for activity

All children: Children are likely to use a trial and improvement approach. Encourage them to reason about numbers and to be systematic, e.g. trying all single tables first, then gradually combining single tables. Once a solution has been found, encourage children to use it as a basis for finding more solutions. To help them, discuss the effect of combining two groups of tables – including single ones – or splitting a group into two (respectively decreasing or increasing the total number of places by 2).

Children may find it helpful to manipulate small square tiles representing tables or to draw them on scraps of paper.

Less able: As the numbers of tables are small enough, encourage children to investigate every possible arrangement of tables.

Optional adult input

Work with the More able group. Ask them to explain the strategy they are using to solve the problem. Encourage them to be systematic.

Plenary

1 Focus on problems 1, 3 and 4. For each, ask children to outline their strategies, and to describe and draw their solutions. Congratulate children who have used a reasoned and systematic approach, not just random trials.

During the explanations, discuss:

- the type of numbers generated when tables are arranged singly, in pairs, in 3s . . . (multiples of 4, 6, 8 . . .);
- the fact that each row of tables seats an even number – so, because the sum of even numbers is always even, whatever the arrangement of tables, there can only be an even total number of places;
- the effect on the total number of places of combining two groups of tables, including single tables (the total decreases by 2) or splitting a group into two groups (the total increases by 2).

2 Work through a possible approach for problem 3, such as that given below. Emphasise that there are many possible approaches.

32 children must be seated using 10 tables. How many children could be seated if all 10 tables were arranged singly?

Establish that as 1 table seats 4, then 10 tables would seat 10 × 4 = 40 children.

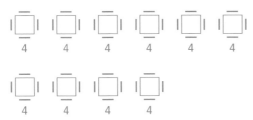

For 10 single tables, total = 40

Establish that we need to reduce the number of places by 40 − 32 = 8.

Ask: *How could we adjust the tables so that they seat 8 fewer children?* Discuss the effect of joining tables – every pair of tables that are joined will reduce the total number of places by 2. So, to reduce the total number of places by 8, we could join 4 pairs of tables.

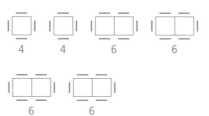

For 2 singles and 4 pairs, total = 32

(A reverse approach would be to start with the 10 tables joined (seating 22) and then gradually separate single tables.)

3 Help children to see that once a successful arrangement has been found it can be rearranged to generate other solutions. Remind them of the effect of combining two groups or splitting a group into two. Ask: *What would be the effect of combining two groups and splitting another group into two groups at the same time?* (The number of places would remain the same.) On this basis, invite children to suggest adjustments to the initial solution for problem 3 that will not affect the total number of places, e.g. combining 2 pairs to make a group of 4 and splitting one of the other pairs into 2 singles to produce:

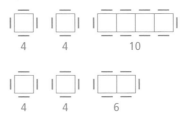

4 singles, 1 pair and 1 group of 4, total = 32

The problems could be 'ongoing' with solutions put on display and added to as new ones are found.

Development

Ask: *What if tables can be in any rectangular arrangement, for example, 2 rows of 3 tables pushed together to seat 10? What other solutions are there to each problem now?*

Solutions

1 2 singles and 1 pair

2 1 single plus 2 pairs; 2 singles plus 1 triple

3 There are several solutions, including:
2 singles plus 4 pairs;
4 singles plus 2 triples;
4 singles, 1 pair and 1 group of 4

4 There are many solutions, including:
1 single, 4 pairs and 2 triples;
2 singles, 2 pairs and 3 triples;
2 singles, 3 pairs, 1 triple and 1 group of 4;
6 singles and 1 group of 9; 6 pairs and 1 triple.

12 Secret code

Minimum prior experience

identification and continuation of shape patterns and sequences

Resources

Textbook page 15, PCM 6, PCM 7 (with the two parts separated), enlarged copy of the letter blanks from PCM 7

Key vocabulary

circle, next, consecutive, adjacent, sequence, predict, pattern, rule

What's the problem?

Children are asked to crack a code in which letters are represented by rectangles divided into 6 squares and shaded in various ways. This involves identifying the rule for a sequence from one or more given elements in the sequence. Children then decode a message.

Problem solving objective

- Solve mathematical problems or puzzles, recognise and explain patterns and relationships, generalise and predict.

Differentiation

More able: Textbook page 15.

Average: Textbook page 15 (same problem but with discretionary clues from PCM 7).

Less able: PCM 6 (similar problem but with more guidance).

Introducing the problem

Ask children for examples of codes they are familiar with, e.g. bar codes, codes for programming a video recorder, ISBN codes for books, Morse code. Discuss how Braille is a form of code in which raised dots on paper represent letters that enable blind people to read. Talk about the use of codes in wartime, and by spies, to enable people on one 'side' to communicate with each other without the other 'side' being able to understand. Explain that code breakers were employed to try to 'crack' the other 'side's' code.

Explain that another sort of code is semaphore, which was useful in the past where there was no other form of communication. In semaphore, two flags are held in different positions to represent different letters. So it can only be used where the two people communicating can see each other (perhaps through binoculars or a telescope).

Explain that today's problem is to crack a flag code in which a different flag represents a different letter of the alphabet, and to read a message in the code.

Teacher focus for activity

More able and Average: Encourage children to work out the complete alphabet using the letter blanks on PCM 7. As they become sure of letters they can substitute them into the message.

As soon as children identify this flag as representing B, confirm that it is.

This should enable them to identify letters up to F:

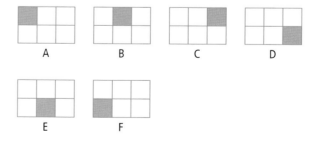

At this stage discuss what children think will represent G. *How many squares do you think will be coloured? Will the squares be joined or separated?* (joined) *Why?* (There are no instances in the message of separated shaded squares.)

Once G and H flags have been established, finding the remaining letters should be relatively straightforward.

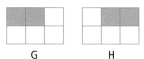

If after some time children are making no headway, offer them some or all of the clues from PCM 7.

Less able: Help children to analyse the sequence of flags by asking questions such as: *How many squares are shaded in letters up to F? How does the sequence go? What happens then? What happens from G to H? What will happen at I? . . .*

Optional adult input

Work with the Less able group and ask children questions about the sequence, such as those suggested above.

Plenary

Display a large copy of the letter blanks from PCM 7. Draw dashes (but not the letters) to represent the coded words on Textbook page 15 and PCM 6.

S T A R   C O D E   B R E A K E R!
B R I L L I A N T!

1 Shade the top left square of the first rectangle to represent A. Invite children to write the As in the words.

2 Ask children to give the flag for B. Discuss what their thoughts were when they were working. Ask: *What else could the flag have been?* (e.g. a square shaded below the top left one) Establish that for the Textbook problem, there were not enough clues to be certain about anything at this stage.

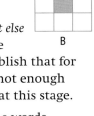

Invite children to write the Bs in the words.

3 Invite children to describe the sequence to F (single squares shaded in a clockwise direction starting at the top left). Invite children to give the flags for each of the letters from C to F in turn, and to write the letters in the words.

4 Ask children to describe the sequence of letters from G to L (blocks of two adjacent squares moving in a clockwise direction). Invite children to describe their thinking before they arrived at this sequence. Invite children to give the flags for each of the letters from G to L in turn and to write the letters in the words.

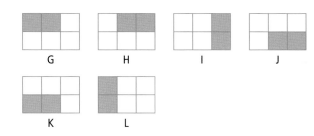

5 Deal with the sequences of letters from M to R, from S to X and from Y to Z in a similar way.

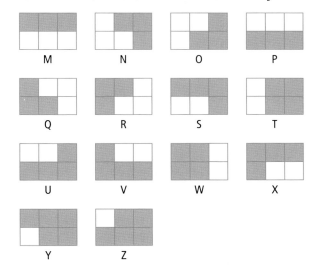

6 Invite children to give you the rule for the whole sequence (e.g. single squares are shaded in a clockwise direction all the way round; then double adjacent squares are shaded all the way round; then triple adjacent squares; then adjacent 4s; then adjacent 5s).

Ask: *If there were more than 26 letters in the alphabet, what would the next five flags be?* Discuss children's responses. Establish that there can be four more blocks of 5 adjacent squares. The final possibility is for all squares to be coloured.

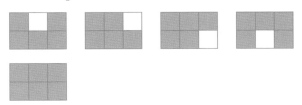

Development

Children could use the code to write messages to each other, or they could make up their own codes.

Solutions

Textbook page 15
STAR CODE BREAKER!

PCM 6
1 See **Plenary** for full alphabet.
2 BRILLIANT!

13 Palindromic investigation

13 Palindromic investigation

A **palindrome** is a word or number that reads the same forwards and backwards. These are **palindromic numbers**:

77   99   131   464   7227   9009   37573

Choose a number: 29
Reverse the digits: 92
Add the two numbers.
The answer is a **palindrome**.
We reached a palindrome in one stage (one addition).

$$\begin{array}{r} 29 \\ + 92 \\ \hline 121 \end{array}$$

Choose a number: 84
Reverse the digits: 48
Add the two numbers.
The answer is **not** a **palindrome**.
Reverse the digits of the total.
Add the two numbers.
The answer **is** a **palindrome**.
We reached a palindrome in two stages (two additions).

$$\begin{array}{r} 84 \\ + 48 \\ \hline 132 \\ + 231 \\ \hline 363 \end{array}$$

16

Minimum prior experience

addition of two numbers less than 500

Resources

Textbook pages 16 and 17, small 100 squares (PCM 8), large 100 square (optional), calculators (discretionary)

Key vocabulary

add, addition, answer, sum, total, palindrome, palindromic, reverse, digit, investigate

What's the problem?

A number is chosen, the digits are reversed to make a new number, then the two numbers are added. If the answer is not a palindromic number, the process is repeated until a palindromic number is produced. Children investigate the production of palindromes in this way for numbers to 100. The investigation involves addition of 2-, 3- and 4-digit numbers (with discretionary use of a calculator).

Problem solving objectives

- Choose and use . . . appropriate ways of calculating to solve problems.
- Explain methods and reasoning about numbers orally and in writing.
- Solve mathematical problems or puzzles, recognise and explain patterns and relationships, generalise and predict.

Differentiation

All children read Textbook page 16, then work from page 17.

More able: problem 3.

Average: problem 3 (same problem with differentiation in the methods used and by outcome).

Less able: problems 1 and 2 (similar problem but with limited investigation).

Introducing the problem

Establish that a palindrome is a word that reads the same forwards or backwards. Write some examples (e.g. 'mum', 'dad', 'toot' and 'deed'), and then invite children to give others.

Explain that numbers can also be palindromic. Write some examples (e.g. 55, 99, 262, 6446, 34143), and then invite children to give others.

Discuss Textbook page 16, ensuring that children understand the procedure for producing palindromes from a starting number. Explain that they will be investigating how many stages it takes for different numbers to produce a palindrome. Point out that they need not investigate numbers that are already palindromes (they reach a palindrome in zero stages).

Teacher focus for activity

All children: Discuss children's methods of addition. They should be able to carry out many of the additions mentally.

Children may need reassuring that multiples of 10 can be included in the investigation. Help them to see that, e.g. 20 added to its reversal is 20 + 02 which is equivalent to 20 + 2 = 22.

More able and Average: Encourage children to work systematically and efficiently, e.g. each child in a pair could investigate a different range of numbers. Ask: *Will you need to reverse and add for every number from 1 to 100?* (No. The reverse of a number already investigated will produce the same result; some numbers are already palindromic.)

Encourage children to think carefully about how they will record their results (perhaps using a table or a 100 square).

69, 78, 79, 87, 96 and 97 involve additions of numbers greater than 1000. In these cases, use your discretion as to whether to allow the use of calculators. 89 and 98 involve 24 additions and result in extremely large numbers, so it is recommended that children leave them until the end or, after trying a few additions, categorise them as 'more than 6 stages'.

Optional adult input

Work with the Average group. Ask children to explain how they are recording their investigation. As they work, ask them to explain their methods of addition for various sums.

Plenary

1 Invite children to explain and show how they recorded their results. They could be categorised under headings (zero-stage numbers, 1-stage numbers, 2-stage numbers . . .) or entered into a table. Alternatively a 100 square could be used with the number of stages for each number indicated in some way, perhaps using a colour code. Congratulate children whose results are recorded clearly.

2 **Draw this table (but not including the numbers).**

number of stages	numbers
0	1, 2, 3, 4, 5, 6, 7, 8, 9, 11, 22, 33, 44, 55, 66, 77, 88, 99
1	10, 12, 13, 14, 15, 16, 17, 18, 20, 21, 23, 24, 25, 26, 27, 29, 30, 31, 32, 34, 35, 36, 38, 40, 41, 42, 43, 45, 47, 50, 51, 52, 53, 54, 56, 60, 61, 62, 63, 65, 70, 71, 72, 74, 80, 81, 83, 90, 92, 100
2	19, 28, 37, 39, 46, 48, 49, 57, 58, 64, 67, 73, 75, 76, 82, 84, 85, 91, 93, 94
3	59, 68, 86, 95
4	69, 78, 87, 96
5	
6	79, 97
more than 6	89, 98

Invite children to give you the numbers for each row. Occasionally go over the additions involved and discuss the methods used. As each number is entered, establish that the reverse of the number can be written in the same row, e.g. 16 and 61. Raise issues as follows:

- **'0-stage' numbers** (i.e. those that are already palindromic)
  Establish that palindromic numbers less than 100 are either single-digit numbers or those whose two digits are the same.

- **'1-stage' numbers**
  Ask: *Which of these numbers give a 2-digit answer? What is special about the numbers that give a 2-digit answer?* Establish that the sum of their digits is less than 10 – those numbers with digit totals of more than 9 cross the tens boundary and result in 'hundreds', e.g. 29 (29 + 92 = 121).

- **'2-stage' numbers**
  Ask: *Do any of these numbers produce a 2-digit answer after the first addition?* (No, because the sum of the digits of each number is greater than 9.) See **Useful mathematical information**, page 90 for more about the sums of digits.

- **'3- and 4-stage' numbers**
  There are only 4 of each.

- **'5-stage' numbers**
  There are none.

- **'6-stage' numbers**
  There are only 2.

- **'More than 6-stage' numbers**
  The only remaining numbers are 89 and 98. Children will probably not have got further than working out that the number of stages is greater than 6. They may be interested to know that the palindrome 8 813 200 023 188 is produced after 24 stages.

Development

Children investigate 3-digit numbers in a similar way.

Solutions

1 1-stage: 18, 26, 38, 45, 53, 65
2-stage: 64, 76, 85, 94

2 See the table in the **Plenary** for more 1- and 2-stage numbers.

3 Investigations will vary. The table in the **Plenary** provides a summary of results.

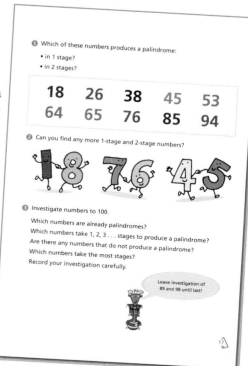

❶ Which of these numbers produces a palindrome:
- in 1 stage?
- in 2 stages?

| 18 | 26 | **38** | 45 | 53 |
| 64 | 65 | 76 | **85** | 94 |

❷ Can you find any more 1-stage and 2-stage numbers?

❸ Investigate numbers to 100.
Which numbers are already palindromes?
Which numbers take 1, 2, 3 . . . stages to produce a palindrome?
Are there any numbers that do not produce a palindrome?
Which numbers take the most stages?
Record your investigation carefully.

Leave investigation of 89 and 98 until last!

14 Windows

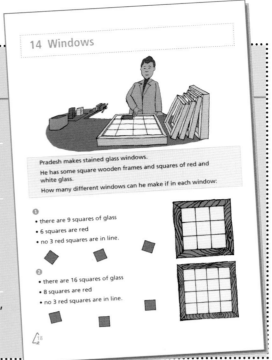

What's the problem?

A square window is made from a grid of smaller red and white square panes. Children investigate the different windows that could be made using a given number of red panes, without forming a line of 3 of them. Potentially the investigation involves systematic working and considerations of symmetry and rotation.

Problem solving objective

- Solve mathematical problems or puzzles, recognise and explain patterns and relationships, generalise and predict. Suggest extensions by asking 'What if . . .?'

Differentiation

All children work from Textbook page 18.

More able: problem 2.

Average: problem 2 (same problem; differentiation in methods used and by outcome).

Less able: problem 1 (similar but simpler investigation).

Introducing the problem

Discuss stained glass windows that children have seen, e.g. in churches or in houses. You could briefly describe how separate pieces of glass are normally enclosed by lead strips.

Look at each problem and make sure children understand what they need to find out (basically they need to find all the different arrangements for 6 or 8 red squares in a grid so that no 3 of them are in line horizontally, vertically or diagonally).

Tell children to record all the possibilities they find using PCM 9 or squared paper, and to write briefly about how they set about the investigation.

Teacher focus for activity

All children: Children may find it helpful to manipulate red counters or small cubes on grids.

Ask: *How many red squares must there be in each row or column?* (2) *Why?* (more than 2 is not allowed; for less than 2, there would need to be more than 2 in one or more of the other rows, to make a total of 6 or 8). Once children understand this, encourage them to work systematically, e.g. fixing the position of 2 red squares in the left of the top row and investigating all possibilities for the other red squares; then repeating for red squares fixed in the first and last squares in the top row . . . They should record all their trials to avoid repetition.

At some stage, depending upon the ability of the children, the issue of whether reflections and rotations should be considered as different may arise. Discuss this. Remind children that the investigation is about windows that can be turned around and turned over.

Optional adult input

Work with the Less able group. Help children to work systematically as described in **Teacher focus for activity**.

Plenary

Display a large copy of PCM 9.

1 Focus on problem 1. Invite children from the Less able group to show their solutions and to describe their method of investigation. Did they just try different arrangements or did they have a fairly systematic method? (e.g. fixing the position of 2 red squares and investigating all the possibilities for the remaining 4 red squares; then repeating for 2 red squares fixed in a different position . . .) Congratulate children who were systematic in some way.

(For the importance of systematic methods when investigating all possibilities, and for a systematic approach to this investigation that you may wish to go over with the class, see **Useful mathematical information** pages 85 and 90–91.)

Establish that these are the only possible arrangements of 6 red squares:

Discuss whether these windows are different or not. For example, rotating either window through a quarter turn clockwise or anticlockwise will produce the same arrangement as on the other window. Alternatively, one window is a reflection of the other. If one window is flipped over, the arrangement of squares can be seen to be the same – you could demonstrate this with a grid copied onto acetate. Establish that since the two windows are in fact the same, strictly speaking there is only one solution.

(See **Useful mathematical information**, page 91 for more about rotations and reflections.)

2 Deal with problem 2 in a similar way. This time there are many more possibilities. Ask children to identify and eliminate those arrangements that are just rotations or reflections of existing solutions. Rotate or flip acetate grids to confirm 'duplicate' windows, e.g.

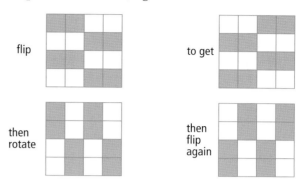

Establish that 4 different windows are possible (see **Solutions**).

Development

More able and Average: *What if each window has 25 small panes, 10 of which are red?*

Less able: *What if there are only 5 red squares for each window?*

Solutions

1 There is just 1 solution. Any other is a reflection/rotation of this.

2 There are just 4 solutions. All others are reflections or rotations of these.

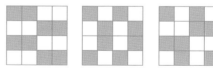

15 Number neighbours

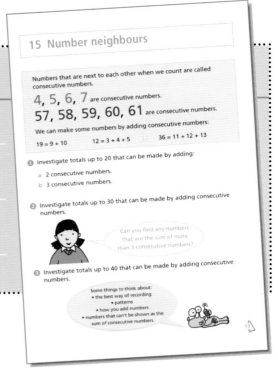

What's the problem?

Investigating which numbers can be expressed as the sum of consecutive numbers. It entails mental addition of 2 or more numbers to 40, and it may involve mental multiplication and division, reasoning about numbers, systematic working, identifying patterns and an understanding of properties of odd and even numbers.

Problem solving objectives

- Choose and use . . . appropriate ways of calculating to solve problems.
- Solve mathematical problems or puzzles, recognise and explain patterns and relationships, generalise and predict. Suggest extensions by asking 'What if . . .?'
- Make and investigate a general statement about familiar numbers or shapes by finding examples that satisfy it.

Differentiation

More able: Textbook page 19, problem 3 (investigating numbers to 40).

Average: Textbook page 19, problem 2 (same problem but with numbers to 30).

Less able: Textbook page 19, problem 1 (similar problem with numbers to 20).

Differentiation will also be by reasoning used.

Introducing the problem

Use the introduction on Textbook page 19 to revise or introduce 'consecutive numbers'. Explain how some numbers can be expressed as the sum of 2 or more consecutive numbers. Ask children to give sets of consecutive numbers and their sums, encouraging the more able to offer 2- or 3-digit consecutive numbers. Discuss mental methods of finding the sums, e.g. 2 consecutive numbers can be regarded as a near double.

Explain that children are asked to find out all that they can about sums of consecutive numbers with totals in their range. Tell them that they should not include zero.

Teacher focus for activity

All children: Encourage children to investigate numbers systematically and to record their results clearly, perhaps in a table. Discuss methods of mental addition, e.g. to add 3 consecutive numbers, just multiply the middle number by 3.

Average and More able: Discuss ways of organising the investigation, e.g. if working in a pair or small group, they could split the number range between them. Encourage children to reason about numbers by asking, e.g. *How could you estimate which 2 (3, 4 . . .) consecutive numbers might add up to this number?* Also encourage them to consider the sums of odd and even numbers: *Are 2 consecutive numbers odd or even?* (one is odd and one is even) *What can you say about the sum of any odd and even number?* (it's odd) *So could this number be expressed as the sum of 2 consecutive numbers?*

Less able: Encourage children to investigate whether there is more than one way of expressing each number as the sum of consecutive numbers (there is for 9, 15 and 18).

Optional adult input

Work with the More able group. Ask children to explain their methods of adding 1, 2, 3, 4 . . . consecutive numbers.

Plenary

1 Invite children to describe their methods of investigation. Congratulate those who worked systematically, e.g.

- dealing with each number in order;

- systematically finding all possible sums of 2 consecutive numbers (1 + 2 = 3; 2 + 3 = 5; 3 + 4 = 7 . . .), then investigating sums of 3, 4 . . . consecutive numbers. (See **Useful mathematical information**, page 92 for a table for numbers to 40 using this approach.)

2 **Draw this table for, say, numbers to 30:**

number	consecutive sums
1	
2	

Invite children to give you sums of consecutive numbers that equal each number in turn. What methods did children use to add 2, 3, 4 . . . consecutive numbers? e.g.

- regarding the sum of 2 consecutive numbers as a near double and adjusting (e.g. 15 + 16 = 15 + 15 + 1 = 31);

- regarding the sum of 3 consecutive numbers as 3 times the middle number (e.g. 12 + 13 + 14 = 3 × 13 = 39).

3 Discuss how children estimated which consecutive numbers might total a particular number. For example: for 2 consecutive numbers, finding 2 that are roughly half the target number (e.g. for 29: 14 and 15); for 3 consecutive numbers, dividing the target number by 3 to provide the middle number (e.g. 30 ÷ 3 = 10, so the numbers are 9, 10 and 11).

4 As the table is completed, encourage children to make observations, e.g.

- The sum of 2 consecutive numbers is always odd. *Why?* (One number is always odd, the other even, and the sum of an odd and an even number is always odd.)

- The sum of 4 consecutive numbers is always even. *Why?* (2 of the numbers are always odd (even sum), 2 are always even (even sum), resulting in an even total.)

- The sum of 3 consecutive numbers can be odd or even. *When will it be odd?* (when the first number is even) *When will it be even?* (when the first number is odd) *Can you explain why?*

- 1, 2, 4, 8, 16, 32 . . . cannot be made by adding consecutive numbers. *What is special about the numbers?* (Each number is double the previous number.)

(See **Useful mathematical information**, page 92 for more observations.)

Development

Children find the 5 sets of consecutive numbers whose sum is 45 (22 and 23; 14, 15 and 16; 7 to 11; 5 to 10; 1 to 9).

Solutions

Here is the full set of results for numbers to 40. Children should not be expected to find them all.

number	consecutive sums
1	
2	
3	1 + 2
4	
5	2 + 3
6	1 + 2 + 3
7	3 + 4
8	
9	4 + 5; 2 + 3 + 4
10	1 + 2 + 3 + 4
11	5 + 6
12	3 + 4 + 5
13	6 + 7
14	2 + 3 + 4 + 5
15	7 + 8; 4 + 5 + 6; 1 + 2 + 3 + 4 + 5
16	
17	8 + 9
18	5 + 6 + 7; 3 + 4 + 5 + 6
19	9 + 10
20	2 + 3 + 4 + 5 + 6
21	10 + 11; 6 + 7 + 8; 1 + 2 + 3 + 4 + 5 + 6
22	4 + 5 + 6 + 7
23	11 + 12
24	7 + 8 + 9
25	12 + 13; 3 + 4 + 5 + 6 + 7
26	5 + 6 + 7 + 8
27	13 + 14; 8 + 9 + 10; 2 + 3 + 4 + 5 + 6 + 7
28	1 + 2 + 3 + 4 + 5 + 6 + 7
29	14 + 15
30	9 + 10 + 11; 6 + 7 + 8 + 9; 4 + 5 + 6 + 7 + 8
31	15 + 16
32	
33	16 + 17; 10 + 11 + 12; 3 + 4 + 5 + 6 + 7 + 8
34	7 + 8 + 9 +10
35	17 + 18; 5 + 6 + 7 + 8 + 9; 2 + 3 + 4 + 5 + 6 + 7 + 8
36	11 + 12 + 13; 1 + 2 + 3 + 4 + 5 + 6 + 7 + 8
37	18 + 19
38	8 + 9 + 10 + 11
39	19 + 20; 12 + 13 + 14; 4 + 5 + 6 + 7 + 8 + 9
40	6 + 7 + 8 + 9 + 10

16 PE purchases

Minimum prior experience

addition of money with 25p, 50p and 75p as the pence component

Resources

Textbook page 20, PCM 10 with clues detached, coins

Key vocabulary

add, sum, total amount, pence, pounds, cost, multiply

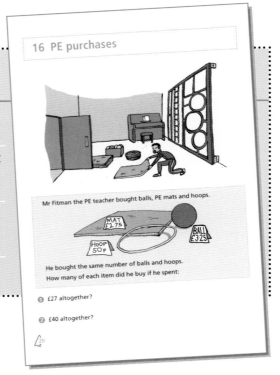

16 PE purchases

Mr Fitman the PE teacher bought balls, PE mats and hoops.

MAT £2.75
HOOP 50P
BALL £3.25

He bought the same number of balls and hoops.
How many of each item did he buy if he spent:

1 £27 altogether?

2 £40 altogether?

20

What's the problem?

Children solve problems in the context of money, using addition and multiplication. Problems may involve using trial and improvement methods or working systematically.

Problem solving objectives

● Choose and use appropriate number operations and appropriate ways of calculating to solve problems.

● Explain methods and reasoning about numbers orally and in writing.

● Use all four operations to solve word problems involving numbers in 'real life' and money, using one or more steps, including converting pounds to pence and vice versa.

Differentiation

More able: Textbook page 20, problem 2.

Average: Textbook page 20, problem 1 (similar but slightly easier problem with a discretionary clue on PCM 10; differentiation is also by methods used).

Less able: PCM 10 (straightforward calculations using the same data).

Introducing the problem

Talk about the problem using Textbook page 20 and PCM 10. Establish the context of the problem (a PE teacher buying PE equipment) and the cost of each item. Use the data as a basis for some simple practice questions, e.g. *What is the cost of 2 balls? . . . 10 hoops? . . . a ball and a hoop? . . . a ball and a PE mat?* Occasionally ask children to explain their methods of mental calculation. Allow the class time to read through their problems and to ask questions before they start.

Teacher focus for activity

All children: Discuss methods of calculation (the 25p, 50p and 75p components of each price make them ideal for mental calculation).

More able and Average: A likely initial approach is to try different numbers of balls and hoops and to see if the remaining amount can be made up with the cost of PE mats. This can be a lengthy 'hit or miss' approach with no guarantee of a solution.

If children continue to work in this way, encourage them to at least list the cost of 1, 2, 3, 4 . . . PE mats so that they are not needlessly repeating calculations.

Children from the Average group could be given the clues from the bottom of PCM 10.

Less able: Children could use coins to help them.

Use coins to ensure that they understand that 75p and 25p make £1, two 50ps make £1, and 75p and 75p make £1.50.

Optional adult input

Work with the Less able group. Ask children to explain their methods of calculation. Help them as described above.

Plenary

1 Focus on the problems on Textbook page 20. Explain that children who did PCM 10 will be able to join in, as the items and prices are the same.

As aide-memoires, write: 'Same number of balls and hoops'; the cost of each item (ball: £3.25; PE mat: £2.75; hoop: 50p); the two total costs (£27 and £40).

Invite children to give their solutions and to explain the problem solving strategies they used. Congratulate children who were systematic in some way and reasoned about numbers.

2 Work through the systematic approach below, which children might have used to some extent.

Draw these tables (with just the headings).

balls and hoops (number of each)	1	2	3	4	5	6	7	8
cost	£3.75	£7.50	£11.25	£15.00	£18.75	£22.50	£26.25	£30.00

PE mats	1	2	3	4	5	6	7	8
cost	£2.75	£5.50	£8.25	£11.00	£13.75	£16.50	£19.25	£22.00

Invite children to calculate the cost of 1 ball and 1 hoop. Enter £3.75 in the first table. Now ask children to calculate the total cost for each of the other numbers. Encourage children from the Less able group to contribute, perhaps using their completed tables from PCM 10 to help with calculations. Each time discuss methods of mental calculation, e.g. to calculate the cost of:

- **2 of each item**
  Double £3 = £6 and double 75p = £1.50
  So, double £3.75 = £6 + £1.50 = £7.50

- **4 of each item**
  Double the cost of 2 of each item (£7.50):
  Double £7 = £14 and double 50p = £1
  So, double £7.50 = £15.00

- **5 of each item**
  Add the cost of 1 of each to the cost of 4 of each:
  £3.75 + £15 = £18.75

Deal with the 'PE mats' table in a similar way. As amounts are entered, ask children to indicate when they think a solution to each problem is apparent. When they do, discuss their reasons. Establish that finding each solution is a matter of identifying an amount from each table with a joint total of £27 or £40. Discuss what to look out for in a pair of amounts, e.g. as each total is a whole number of pounds, then each amount must be a whole number of pounds, or the pence components of both amounts must add up to a pound (e.g. 50p and 50p; 25p and 75p).

Finally establish that:
  5 balls, 5 hoops and 3 PE mats cost £27;
  7 balls, 7 hoops and 5 PE mats cost £40.

3 Ask: *Could there be more than one solution for each problem?* (Yes)

Establish that to find out, the tables need to be extended and other pairs of amounts across tables need to be checked for sums of £27 and £40 (See **Useful mathematical information**, page 92 for extended tables.)

Development

Children investigate whether there is more than one solution to each problem. (there isn't)

Solutions

Textbook page 20

1 5 balls, 5 hoops and 3 PE mats

2 7 balls, 7 hoops and 5 PE mats

PCM 10

1a

number of hoops	1	2	3	4	5
cost	50p	£1.00	£1.50	£2.00	£2.50

b

number of balls	1	2	3	4	5
cost	£3.25	£6.50	£9.75	£13.00	£16.25

c

number of PE mats	1	2	3	4	5
cost	£2.75	£5.50	£8.25	£11.00	£13.75

2a £3.75   b £11.25   c £6.00   d £18.00   e £19.50

17 Area challenge

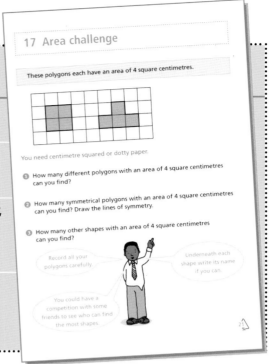

17 Area challenge

These polygons each have an area of 4 square centimetres.

You need centimetre squared or dotty paper.

1. How many different polygons with an area of 4 square centimetres can you find?

2. How many symmetrical polygons with an area of 4 square centimetres can you find? Draw the lines of symmetry.

3. How many other shapes with an area of 4 square centimetres can you find?

Record all your polygons carefully.

Underneath each shape write its name if you can.

You could have a competition with some friends to see who can find the most shapes.

Minimum prior experience

finding area by counting squares

Resources

Textbook page 21, centimetre squared or dotty paper, tracing paper, pin boards, mirrors, write-on display grid of squares

Key vocabulary

area, square centimetre (cm²), covers, symmetrical, line symmetry, line of symmetry, reflect, reflection, 2-D shape names, polygon, pin board

What's the problem?

Children find all the shapes they can with an area of 4 square centimetres, naming the shapes and identifying those that are symmetrical. Shapes may include ones that enclose fractions of squares.

Problem solving objective

- Solve mathematical problems or puzzles, recognise and explain patterns and relationships, generalise and predict. Suggest extensions by asking 'What if . . .?'

Differentiation

All children work from Textbook page 21. Differentiation will be mainly by outcome.

More able and Average: problems 2 and 3.

Less able: problems 1 and 2 (essentially the same problems but in a different order).

Introducing the problem

Display a large write-on grid of squares. If the squares are not centimetre squares, ask children to imagine that they are. Invite 4 children to each draw a polygon with an area of 5 square centimetres (5 cm²), e.g.

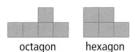

octagon   hexagon

Confirm that each shape covers 5 centimetre squares (or the equivalent, if the shape encloses fractions of squares). Invite children to name the polygons where

possible (if necessary revise the names of polygons such as pentagon, quadrilateral, octagon . . .).

Invite children to identify which shapes (if any) are symmetrical and to draw their lines of symmetry (mirror lines). If none of the shapes are symmetrical, then invite children to draw one that is.

Explain that the investigation is about finding shapes with an area of 4 square centimetres. Remind children to record each polygon carefully and, if possible, to write its name. Suggest that they might like to compete with a partner to see who can find the most shapes.

Teacher focus for activity

All children: Ask children to demonstrate that the area of each shape they have drawn is 4 cm². Look out for children who are counting identical shapes, that have just been rotated, as being different. Show why they are the same by getting children to trace one of the shapes if necessary and turning it on top of the other.

 rotated through a quarter turn clockwise gives

Encourage children to consider shapes that cover fractions of squares. Many children will be able to explore no further than half single squares, but children from the More able group may be able to consider half of rectangles made up of 2 or more squares.

56

The area of the triangle is half the area of the rectangle.
So, area of triangle = half of 2 cm² = 1 cm²

Encourage children to be as specific as possible when naming shapes, e.g. 'isosceles triangle' or 'right-angled triangle', rather than just 'triangle'.

Children may find it helpful to use a pin board to investigate shapes before committing them to paper. They may also find it helpful to use a mirror to identify lines of symmetry.

Children could check each other's shapes.

Optional adult input

Work with the Average group. Ask children to demonstrate that their shapes have an area of 4 square centimetres. Ask them to justify lines of symmetry, perhaps using a mirror.

Plenary

1 Display a large write-on grid of squares. If the squares are not centimetre squares, ask children to imagine that they are.

   Invite children to draw polygons on the grid that have an area of 4 square centimetres, but only shapes with all sides along the grid lines. Encourage the Less able group to contribute at this stage in particular.

   Establish that shapes that are rotations of one another are the same shapes. You could debate whether reflections (that are not also rotations) are different, e.g.

   (For more about this see **Useful mathematical information**, page 91.)

   Including reflections, 7 shapes with sides along the grid lines have an area of 4 square centimetres:

   Invite children to identify which polygons are symmetrical and to draw any lines of symmetry. Also invite children to give a name to each shape (octagon, hexagon, square or rectangle).

2 Invite children to draw symmetrical polygons with areas of 4 square centimetres that contain oblique lines (lines that are not along the grid lines). Ask them to show that the area of their shape is 4 square centimetres. Help children to 'see' oblique lines as dividing a rectangle in half, e.g.

   area of triangle = ½ of 2 cm²   area of triangle = ½ of 3 cm²
                    = 1 cm²   = 1½ cm²

   area of triangle = ½ of 4 cm²
                    = 2 cm²

   Ask children to draw in any lines of symmetry. Discuss the names of the shapes, e.g. isosceles triangle, right-angled triangle, oblong or rectangle, quadrilateral.

   Children could cross off each shape on their own recordings as it is drawn.

3 If time allows continue in a similar way with non-symmetrical polygons.

Development

Children investigate shapes with an area of 5 cm².

Solutions

1 See 3 below. Expect only shapes with all sides along grid lines.

2 Here are some symmetrical shapes. Others are possible. Lines of symmetry are shown. For the Less able group, expect only shapes with all sides along grid lines.

   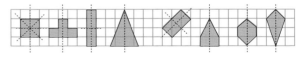

3 Here are some alternative shapes. Others are possible.

18 Dog run

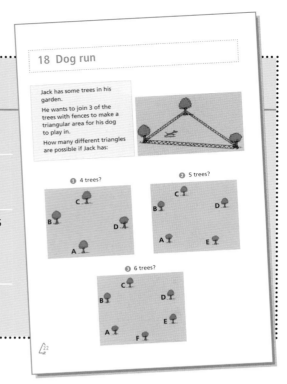

Minimum prior experience

identifying triangles

Resources

Textbook pages 22 and 23, pentagonal and hexagonal pin boards (optional)

Key vocabulary

pattern, predict, triangle, quadrilateral, vertex, sequence, justify, combination, systematic

What's the problem?

Children find how many different triangular or quadrilateral areas can be formed by joining trees with fences. This involves systematic working to identify all possible outcomes in a situation.

Problem solving objectives

- Explain methods and reasoning about numbers orally and in writing.
- Solve mathematical problems or puzzles, recognise and explain patterns and relationships, generalise and predict. Suggest extensions by asking 'What if . . .?'
- Make and investigate a general statement about familiar numbers or shapes by finding examples that satisfy it.

Differentiation

More able: Textbook page 23, problem 4 (making quadrilaterals with 7 trees).

Average: Textbook page 22, problem 3 (making triangles with 6 trees).

Less able: Textbook page 22, problems 1 and 2 (making triangles with 4, then 5, trees).

Differentiation will also be through methods used.

Introducing the problem

Make sure children understand the problem: a garden has a number of trees in a roughly circular arrangement; an area of garden is fenced off using fences between 3 or 4 of the trees; they must work out how many different areas could be made in this way.

Explain that children should think carefully about the best ways to investigate and to record their findings.

Teacher focus for activity

More able and Average: If children are getting confused recording diagrammatically, discuss how they could use the letters of the trees to record. Encourage children to do this systematically by asking, e.g. *How can you make sure you have found all the triangles? How can you avoid repeating any triangles?*

Average and Less able: Children may find pentagonal or hexagonal pin boards helpful for problems 2 and 3.

Less able: With the relatively small numbers of triangles involved, children may be able to record their answers purely diagrammatically, e.g.

If children are finding this difficult, discuss how triangles can be recorded using the letters of the vertices (trees) – ABC, ABD, ABE . . .

All children: Ask children who are already recording systematically using letters, to describe their method. Have they discovered any patterns?

Optional adult input

Work with the Average group. Ask children to describe their method of investigation. Ask: *How will you know if you have found all possible triangles?*

Freya has 7 trees in her garden.

She wants to join 4 of the trees with fences to make a quadrilateral area for her dog to play in.

How many different quadrilaterals are possible?

Plenary

1 Invite children from each group to give their solution and to describe their method of investigation. They may have investigated and recorded: using diagrams; using letters; systematically; randomly.

Can children say with confidence that they have found the maximum number of possible triangles or quadrilaterals? Can they justify this? Discuss how systematic working ensures that all possible shapes are found.

(For the importance of working systematically see **Useful mathematical information**, page 85.)

2 Work through problem 3 on Textbook page 22 using the following systematic approach.

Draw 6 dots in a roughly circular arrangement. Label them A to F.

Explain that you are going to fix one point and find all possible triangles with that vertex. Join A to B, B to C, and C to A.

Establish this as the first triangle. Write ABC. Make sure children understand the representation of a triangle in this way.

Discuss which triangles could be identified next. Establish that one systematic way would be to find

all the triangles with side AB. Invite children to draw and list them: (ABC), ABD, ABE, ABF

With vertex A still fixed, discuss which triangles could be listed next. Establish that it would seem sensible to find all possible 'AC' triangles. Invite children to give the 'AC' triangles that are not repeats of previous triangles. Draw and list them: ACD, ACE and ACF.

Continue in a similar way with the 'AD' and 'AE' triangles. Establish that all triangles that include point (tree) A have been found. Point out that we can be confident about this because we have worked systematically (identifying them in order).

Which point shall we fix next? Establish that B would be a systematic choice. Ask children to name all the 'B' triangles. At this stage, many children should be able to use the pattern of letters to help them find the triangles, rather than referring to a diagram. Establish BCD, BCE, BCF, BDE, BDF and BEF as the 'B' triangles.

ABC	ABD	ABE	ABF	ACD	ACE	ACF	ADE	ADF	AEF
			BCD	BCE	BCF	BDE	BDF	BEF
Listing the triangles like this					CDE	CDF	CEF
will emphasise the sequences.							DEF

Continue in a similar way, fixing points C and D in turn. Establish that once the 'D' triangles have been found, there are no more different triangles – so there are 20 different triangles. Reinforce that you can be confident that you have found them all because you have worked systematically.

Development

Investigate the number of possibilities for:
More able: quadrilaterals with 8 trees.
Average: triangles with 7 trees.
Less able: quadrilaterals with 5 trees.

Solutions

1 4 triangles **2** 10 triangles

3 20 triangles **4** 35 quadrilaterals

(See **Useful mathematical information**, page 93 for all possibilities for problems 1, 2 and 4).

19 Ginger biscuits

Minimum prior experience

multiplying 3-digit numbers by 10; simple addition and subtraction of money

Resources

Textbook pages 24 and 25

Key vocabulary

weight, mass, kilogram, grams, double, multiply, add, total amount, data

19 Ginger biscuits

Each person in a cookery class is going to make 10 ginger biscuits.
The teacher needs to buy the flour, the margarine and the sugar.

Ingredients for 10 ginger biscuits
125 g flour
50 g margarine
75 g sugar
25 ml syrup
1 tsp ground ginger

❶ There are 10 people in the cookery class.
a How much flour will be needed?
b How many bags will the teacher need to buy?

c How much margarine will be needed?
d How many tubs will the teacher need to buy?

e How much sugar will be needed?
f How many bags will the teacher need to buy?

g How much will the teacher pay altogether for the flour, margarine and sugar he buys?
h How much change will he get from £10?

24

What's the problem?

A 'real-life' word problem based on finding the total cost of ingredients required for a cookery class. It involves an ability to work methodically and to identify and use relevant data, addition and multiplication of 2- and 3-digit numbers and amounts of money, and knowledge of the number of grams in a kilogram.

Problem solving objectives

- Choose and use appropriate number operations and appropriate ways of calculating to solve problems.
- Explain methods and reasoning about numbers orally and in writing.
- Use all four operations to solve word problems involving numbers in 'real life', money and measures, using one or more steps, including converting pounds to pence and vice versa.

Differentiation

More able: Textbook page 25, problem 3 (involving multiplying by 25).

Average: Textbook page 25, problem 2 (same problem but involving multiplying by 20).

Less able: Textbook page 24, problem 1 (series of simple questions using the same data).

Introducing the problem

Use the problem introduction on Textbook page 24 to set the scene for the problem: a group of people in a cookery class, each making 10 ginger biscuits. Ask one or two questions about the data, e.g. *How much margarine is there in a tub?* (250 g) *How much does a bag of flour cost?* (72p)

Encourage children to read through their problems carefully. Suggest that, for problems 2 and 3, children work with a partner to develop a strategy for solving the problem. Explain that they should record carefully what they do and their methods of calculation.

Teacher focus for activity

More able and Average: Ask children to explain their problem solving strategies and their methods of calculation. Encourage them to devise mental methods wherever possible, e.g. to multiply by 20: multiply by 10 and double.

Where children are having difficulty in working out a strategy ask 'leading' questions such as:

- *What is the problem asking?* (how much change there will be from £10)
- *What do we need to know before we can work out the change?* (how much was spent)
- *What was the money spent on?* (flour, margarine and sugar)
- *How can we find out how much was spent on flour?* (work out the number of bags bought, then multiply the price by the number of bags)

Use the recipe on page 24 to find out how much change the teacher will get from £10 if:

② there are 20 people in the cookery class.

③ there are 25 people in the cookery class.

Flour is sold in 1.5 kg bags.

A bag of sugar costs 69p.

Sugar is sold in 1 kg bags.

A 250 g tub of margarine costs 75p.

A bag of flour costs 72p.

Less able: You may need to revise multiplication of whole numbers by 10, showing how digits are shifted one place to the left and a zero put at the end to 'hold' the units place. Children may also need reminding of the number of grams in a kilogram.

Optional adult input

Work with the Average group. Ask children to explain their problem solving strategies. For children who are having difficulty, ask 'leading' questions such as those suggested in the **Teacher focus for activity**.

Plenary

1 Focus on problem 3. Explain that all children will be able to join in, as most of the data in each problem is the same.

Briefly read through the problem. Establish that it involves working out the change from £10 after buying the flour, margarine and sugar. Ask children to outline the steps they took (or would take) to solve the problem.

2 Go through the steps one at a time. When appropriate, discuss methods of calculation, encouraging mental methods (some suggestions are given in **Useful mathematical information**, page 93). Steps are likely to be as follows (although they might be done in a different order):

- **Step 1: Calculate the weight of flour needed**
  $125 \text{ g} \times 25 = 3125 \text{ g}$
  or 3 kg 125 g

- **Step 2: Work out how many bags of flour the teacher needs to buy**
  3 bags (which hold a total of $4\frac{1}{2}$ kg) are needed.

- **Step 3: Calculate the cost of the bags of flour**
  $72\text{p} \times 3 = £2.16$

- **Step 4: Calculate the weight of margarine needed**
  $50 \text{ g} \times 25 = 1250 \text{ g}$
  or 1 kg 250 g

- **Step 5: Work out how many tubs of margarine the teacher needs to buy**
  5 tubs (which hold a total of 1 kg 250 g) are needed.

- **Step 6: Calculate the cost of the tubs of margarine**
  $75\text{p} \times 5 = 375\text{p} = £3.75$

- **Step 7: Calculate the weight of sugar needed**
  $75 \text{ g} \times 25 = 1875 \text{ g}$
  or 1 kg 875 g

- **Step 8: Work out how many bags of sugar the teacher needs to buy**
  2 bags (which hold a total of 2 kg) are needed.

- **Step 9: Calculate the cost of the bags of sugar**
  $69\text{p} \times 2 = £1.38$

- **Step 10: Calculate the total cost of the ingredients**
  $£2.16 + £3.75 + £1.38 = £7.29$

- **Step 11: Subtract the total cost of the ingredients from £10**
  $£10 - £7.29 = £2.71$

(Steps for problem 2 are given in **Useful mathematical information**, page 93–94)

Development

Children find a very simple recipe for biscuits or a cake and research the costs of ingredients for different numbers of people.

Solutions

1a 1250 g or 1 kg 250 g	**b** 1 bag
c 500 g	**d** 2 tubs
e 750 g	**f** 1 bag
g £2.91	**h** £7.09

2 £4.18

3 £2.71

20 Wristbands

20 Wristbands

Jack has a bag of beads to make wristbands.

1. With the beads he could make wristbands with:

   2 beads on each but have 1 bead left over
   3 beads on each and have no beads left over
   5 beads on each and have no beads left over
   4 beads on each but have 1 bead left over

   There are fewer than 50 beads in the bag.
   How many beads are there?

2. With the beads he could make wristbands with:

   2 beads on each and have no beads left over
   3 beads on each and have no beads left over
   5 beads on each but have 2 beads left over
   7 beads on each but have 2 beads left over

   There are fewer than 100 beads in the bag.
   How many beads are there?

26

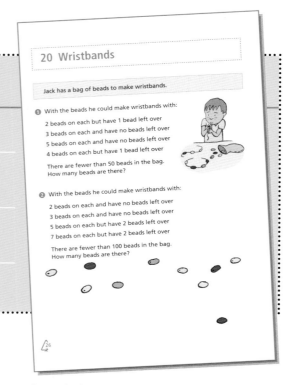

Minimum prior experience

counting in 2s, 3s and 5s

Resources

Textbook page 26, PCM 11, beads or counters

Key vocabulary

odd, even, multiple of, sequence, continue, pattern, divisible by

What's the problem?

Jack has a bag of beads to make wristbands. Children are given information about the number of beads that would be left over if he put a given number of beads on each wristband. They use sequences, multiples and reasoning about numbers to work out how many beads Jack has.

Problem solving objectives

- Explain methods and reasoning about numbers orally and in writing.
- Solve mathematical problems or puzzles, recognise and explain patterns and relationships, generalise and predict. Suggest extensions by asking 'What if . . .?'

Differentiation

More able: Textbook page 26, problem 2.

Average: Textbook page 26, problem 1 (similar but simpler problem).

Less able: PCM 11 (similar but simpler problem, with step by step guidance).

Introducing the problem

Hide 8 beads (or counters) in your hand. *There are fewer than 10 beads in my hand. If I grouped them in 2s, there would be none left over. If I grouped them in 3s, there would be 2 left over. How many beads are in my hand?* (8) Discuss answers. Explain that today's problems are similar but more complicated.

Set the problem context: Jack has a bag of beads with which to make wristbands; he can make wristbands with 2, 3, 4 . . . beads on each and have some, or none, left over. Establish that children are asked to work out how many beads are in the bag from the information given.

Teacher focus for activity

More able and Average: Ask: *What can you tell me about the number of beads in the bag?* (e.g. It's a multiple of 2 and 3 (More able) . . . 3 and 5 (Average).) Ask children to explain their approach to the problem. Encourage them to reason about numbers and to look for efficient ways of finding a solution, e.g. with problem 1: *Is it necessary to list all multiples of 3 and all multiples of 5?* (no, just multiples of 5 that are also multiples of 3 could be listed)

Use a variety of terminology synonymously, e.g. 'divisible by 2', 'multiple of 2', 'even'. Encourage children to reason about numbers, by asking questions such as: *What can you say about numbers that are multiples of both 2 and 3?* (they are multiples of 6)

Less able: With question 4, help children to see that, to meet all three conditions, the number must appear in all three tables that they completed for questions 1 to 3.

Optional adult input

Work with the Less able group. Get children to practice counting in 2s, 3s and 5s. Ask them to identify numbers that are multiples of both 2 and 3 (or 2 and 5, or 3 and 5) and then (for the solution to question 4) 2, 3 and 5.

Plenary

1 Ask children from each group to give their solutions and to describe their methods.

2 Focus on problem 2 on Textbook page 26. **Ensure that all children can see the problem or write it on the board.**

Discuss where to start. The order given here may be different, but the approach should be similar.

Children may suggest listing multiples of 2 and multiples of 3. Establish that listing just multiples of 3 that are also multiples of 2 (even) saves writing two lists. Ask children to give you the numbers (the Less able group could use their tables for questions 1 and 2 on PCM 11 to help them identify the first few):

6   12   18   24   30   36   42   48
54   60   66   72   78   84   90   96

Encourage children to look for patterns as the sequence is written. They may notice the pattern in the units digits (6, 2, 8, 4, 0, 6, 2 . . .) or that multiples of both 2 and 3 are also multiples of 6.

Establish that any number in the sequence could be the number of beads in the bag. *What else do we know about the number of beads?* (It could produce wristbands with 5 beads on each and 2 beads remaining, or wristbands with 7 beads on each and 2 beads remaining.) Establish the need to generate a sequence of possible numbers for each condition. Deal with each in turn, writing the numbers as children give them.

For 5 beads on each wristband and 2 left over, children should quickly realise that the units digits alternate between 2 and 7:

7   12   17   22   27   32   37   42   47   52
57   62   67   72   77   82   87   92   97

Can they explain why? (you are adding 5 each time, so the difference between every other number is 10)

Ask: *Could we discard any numbers in this sequence?* Remind children that the number of beads must be a multiple of 2 and 3 (numbers in the first sequence generated) so any numbers that are not, can be deleted:

~~7~~   12   ~~17~~   ~~22~~   ~~27~~   ~~32~~   ~~37~~   42   ~~47~~   ~~52~~
~~57~~   ~~62~~   ~~67~~   72   ~~77~~   ~~82~~   ~~87~~   ~~92~~   ~~97~~

Establish that the possible solutions have been narrowed down to 12, 42 and 72.

When listing the numbers for 7 beads on each wristband with 2 beads remaining, invite children to say when they think they know the solution to the problem:

9   16   23   30   37   44   51   58
65   72   79   86   93   100

12 and 42 are not in the sequence – only the remaining possibility, 72, is.

Establish that the only number which satisfies all four conditions is 72.

(For more about identification of multiples and rules of divisibility, and also how to use the constant function on a calculator for generating sequences see **Useful mathematical information**, page 94.)

Development

Children investigate which is the next possible number of beads in the bag beyond the limited total given in their problem.

Solutions

Textbook page 26

1   45 beads

2   72 beads

PCM 11

1

wristbands	1	2	3	4	5	6	7	8	9	10	11	12	13	14	15
beads	2	4	6	8	10	12	14	16	18	20	22	24	26	28	30

2

wristbands	1	2	3	4	5	6	7	8	9	10	11	12	13	14	15
beads	3	6	9	12	15	18	21	24	27	30	33	36	39	42	45

3

wristbands	1	2	3	4	5	6	7	8	9	10	11	12	13	14	15
beads	5	10	15	20	25	30	35	40	45	50	55	60	65	70	75

4   30 beads

21 Grid totals

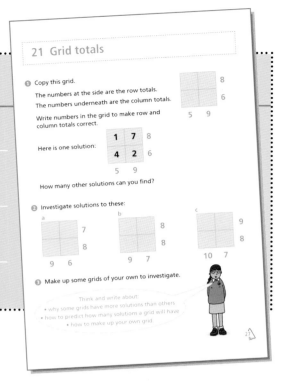

Minimum prior experience

adding single-digit numbers

Resources

Textbook page 27, squared paper

Key vocabulary

add, addition, grid, row, column, sum, total

What's the problem?

Children are given addition grids with row and column totals provided. They investigate numbers that could be placed in the grid to produce those totals. This involves addition of small numbers, reasoning about numbers and could also involve making generalisations and predictions.

Problem solving objectives

- Explain methods and reasoning about numbers orally and in writing.
- Solve mathematical problems or puzzles, recognise and explain patterns and relationships, generalise and predict. Suggest extensions by asking 'What if . . .?'
- Make and investigate a general statement about familiar numbers or shapes by finding examples that satisfy it.

Differentiation

All children work from Textbook page 27. Differentiation will be by outcome (the amount of reasoning used and generalisations made).

Introducing the problem

Draw this addition grid without the column and row totals.

3	8	11
9	5	14
12	13	

Explain that for an addition grid, row totals are put at the ends of the rows and column totals are put underneath the columns. Invite children to provide the totals and write them in.

Explain that in their investigation children are given the row and column totals and are asked to work out what the numbers in the grid could be. Highlight the 'Think and write about' suggestions at the bottom of Textbook page 27.

Teacher focus for activity

All children: The likely initial approach is to focus on any one row or column total; write in two numbers with that total, then attempt to fill in the remaining numbers so that all totals are correct; if that is not possible, then try again. Ask questions such as: *Why didn't this work? Is this the best total to concentrate on?* Children may eventually realise that the smallest total is the most helpful one to concentrate on.

Encourage children to think about what determines the total number of possible solutions (the number of solutions is equal to the number of possible additions for the smallest total).

Ask children to explain how they set about making their own grids.

Less able: Encourage children to systematically write out the addition bonds for any total they are considering (e.g. for 6: 0 + 6, 1 + 5, 2 + 4, 3 + 3, 4 + 2, 5 + 1, 6 + 0).

Optional adult input

Work with the Less able group. Help children to work out the addition bonds for totals as described above.

Plenary

1 Draw this grid.

Invite children to suggest how it might be solved. Children are likely to suggest either:

a choosing any one of the totals, trying addition pairs with that total, and attempting to fill in the remaining numbers in the grid to fit with the other totals

or

b choosing the smallest total, finding pairs with that total and completing the rest of the grid.

2 Try option **a**. Supposing the row total 7 is selected, ask: *Which pairs of numbers have a sum of 7?* Encourage children to give them systematically. List them on the board:

0 and 7, 1 and 6, 2 and 5, 3 and 4, 4 and 3, 5 and 2, 6 and 1, 7 and 0.

Establish that reversals are important because, although they include the same numbers, the numbers will occupy different squares.

Write 0 and 7 in the top row of the grid. *Could 0 and 7 be the two numbers?* (no) *Why not?* Establish that the 7 is too big to be one of the numbers for the column total 5.

Try the next pair of numbers (1 and 6) and establish that the 6 is also too large for the column total 5.

Establish that the first possible pair is 2 and 5. Enter this pair. Invite children to find the other grid numbers and fill them in.

Continue in this way with the other pairs of numbers. At some point, children should realise, or you can elicit from them, that the limiting factor each time is the smallest total (in this case 5). Whichever total is selected, those numbers in the addition pairs that do not 'fit' with the total 5 cannot be in the grid. So it would seem sensible when solving a grid to focus on the smallest total straight away. All the numbers in the pairs for the smallest total are bound to be suitable for the larger totals. (This is the approach **b** that some children may have suggested at the start.)

Work through one or more of the grids on Textbook page 27 using this approach. Focusing immediately on the smallest total, children will find that all pairs of numbers with that sum will fit into the grid and produce all the solutions.

3 *Why do some grids have more solutions than others?* Discuss responses. Establish that the number of solutions is determined by the number of possible pairs that give the smallest total. So, for the introductory grid on Textbook page 27: 5 is the smallest total; there are 6 pairs of numbers that equal it, so there are 6 solutions.

Children may notice that the number of possible pairs for any total is one more than the total. So a grid with 3 as the smallest total will have $3 + 1 = 4$ solutions; a grid with 7 as the smallest total will have $7 + 1 = 8$ solutions . . .

4 *How can you make up your own grid?* Discuss children's suggestions. The crucial factor is that the sum of the row totals must equal the sum of the column totals, otherwise the grid will not 'work'. This is because both the sum of the row totals and the sum of the column totals are essentially the sum of all four grid numbers.

Development

Children investigate 3×3 addition grids (with very small numbers) in a similar way.

Solutions

1 6 solutions in total:

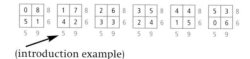

(introduction example)

2a

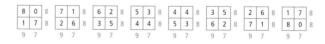

b

c

3 Children's own grids.

22 Quick time

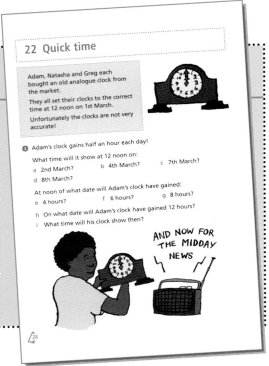

What's the problem?

An analogue clock that gains a given number of minutes each day is set to the correct time at 12 noon on a particular day. Children work out when the clock will next show the correct time. This involves adding and dividing units of time and reasoning about time, and it may involve knowing the number of days in a month.

Problem solving objectives

- Choose and use appropriate number operations and appropriate ways of calculating to solve problems.
- Explain methods and reasoning about numbers orally and in writing.
- Solve mathematical problems or puzzles, recognise and explain patterns and relationships, generalise and predict. Suggest extensions by asking 'What if . . .?'
- Use all four operations to solve word problems involving numbers in 'real life' and measures (including time), using one or more steps.

Differentiation

More able: Textbook page 29, problem 3.

Average: Textbook page 29, problem 2 (similar but slightly simpler problem).

Less able: Textbook page 28, problem 1 (simpler problems in the same context).

Introducing the problem

Ask children with watches to tell the time. Discuss the range of times given. Discuss what powers their watches (probably batteries). Do any children have analogue watches (with hands)?

Talk about how watches and clocks in the past usually were analogue and used a spring mechanism for moving the hands, which needed to be wound up regularly. If a 'wind-up' watch or clock is available, demonstrate this. Explain that such watches and clocks were not as accurate as those today and their hands would often go round slightly too fast (causing them to 'gain' time) or too slow (causing them to 'lose' time). People would talk about their watches or clocks being 'fast' or 'slow'. Ask: *If I have a watch that is 5 minutes fast (has gained 5 minutes) and the time it shows is 6:25, what time is it really?* (6:20) Ask similar questions, including some for watches that are 'slow'.

Explain that today's problems are about old analogue clocks that 'gain' time.

Teacher focus for activity

More able: Ask: *What time will it be when the clock next shows the correct time?* (12 noon – although the clock will 'think' it is 12 midnight)

More able and Average: Check that children know how many minutes there are in an hour and that from noon one day to noon the next is a complete day.

Ask children to explain their strategy. One likely, but long-winded, approach is to work out the time the

2 Natasha's clock gains 15 minutes each day!
On what date will her clock next show 12 o'clock again?

3 Greg's clock gains 10 minutes each day!
On what date will his clock next show the correct time?

29

clock shows at noon each day until it shows 12 o'clock again. Can children think of a quicker method?

Less able: Make sure children can count on in half hours, e.g. 12 noon, 12:30, 1 o'clock, 1:30 . . . Ensure they understand that from noon on one day to noon on the next is a complete day. Ask, e.g. *How many days will it take for the clock to gain 2 ($2\frac{1}{2}$, 3 . . .) hours?* Some children may need to use a clock face with moving hands.

Optional adult input

Work with the Average group. Check that children know relevant facts about time by asking, e.g. *How many minutes are there in an hour? How many hours are there from 12 noon to 12 midnight? How many days are there in March and April? What fraction of an hour is 15 minutes?*

Plenary

1 Focus on **1e**. Invite the Less able group to explain their reasoning. Establish that if the clock gains half an hour each day, it gains an hour every 2 days. So it will gain 4 hours in $4 \times 2 = 8$ days. 8 days from noon on 1st March is noon on 9th March.

Deal with **f** and **g** in a similar way.

For **h**, establish that the clock will gain 12 hours in $12 \times 2 = 24$ days, i.e. at noon on 25th March. Use the clock face to establish that at 12 noon, a clock that has gained 12 hours will show 12 midnight, but with an analogue clock both times look the same.

2 Focus on problem 2. (An alternative plenary (for problem 3) is provided in **Useful mathematical information**, pages 94–95.)

Invite children to give their answers and describe their methods. There are two likely methods:

- Listing days and times shown at noon each day until 12 o'clock appears again (12:00, 12:15, 12:30, 12:45 . . .) is long-winded. A more efficient approach is to reason that the clock gains 1 hour every 4 days, so every 4th day could be listed as showing an increase of 1 hour. If no-one suggests this method you could elicit it from them.

Children will need to know the number of days in March (31) when they cross the March/April boundary. (See **Useful mathematical information**, page 95 for help in remembering how many days are in each month.)

noon on clock time	March 1st	5th	9th	13th	17th	21st	25th	29th	April 2nd	6th	10th	14th	18th
	12:00	1:00	2:00	3:00	4:00	5:00	6:00	7:00	8:00	9:00	10:00	11:00	12:00

The clock will next show 12 o'clock at noon on 18th April.

- Reason that the next time the clock shows 12 o'clock will be when it has gained 12 hours. If the clock gains 1 hour in 4 days, it will gain 12 hours in 12×4 days = 48 days. So you need to count on 48 days from noon on 1st March. Discuss methods of doing this. A calendar could be used, or children might reason that 30 days on from noon on 1st of March brings us to noon on 31st March. There are 18 days remaining from the 48 days, which takes us to noon on 18th April.

Development

Ask: *What if each clock lost 10 (or 15) minutes each day? When would it next show 12 o'clock?*

Solutions

1a 12:30   **b** 1:30   **c** 3:00

  d 3:30   **e** 9th March   **f** 13th March

  g 17th March   **h** 25th March   **i** 12:00

2 18th April

3 12th May

23 Winning totals

23 Winning totals

On these dartboards there are just two numbers.
Use as many darts as you like to get the winning total exactly.
How many different ways can you find?

Minimum prior experience

counting in 3s and 5s; simple mental addition

Resources

Textbook page 30, PCM 12

Key vocabulary

pattern, sequence, multiple of, sum, total, divisible by

What's the problem?

There are two numbers on a dartboard and an unlimited number of darts. Children are asked to find all possible ways of making a given score. These could be found by trial and improvement or through more systematic investigation. Investigations may involve knowledge of 3, 5 and 7 times-tables (or an ability to generate multiples of those numbers), mental addition and reasoning about numbers.

Problem solving objectives

- Choose and use appropriate number operations and appropriate ways of calculating to solve problems.
- Explain methods and reasoning about numbers orally and in writing.
- Solve mathematical problems or puzzles, recognise and explain patterns and relationships, generalise and predict. Suggest extensions by asking 'What if . . .?'

Differentiation

More able: Textbook page 30, problem 2.

Average: Textbook page 30, problem 1 (similar but slightly simpler problem).

Less able: PCM 12 (similar problem but presented in steps).

Introducing the problem

Talk about fairground darts games in which particular scores win a prize. Explain that children's problems are about a similar game, but the dartboard and rules are unusual: there are only 2 numbers on the dartboard and you can use as many darts as you like.

Explain that some scores can be made in more than one way and that you would like children to be sure that they have found all possible ways. They should record what they do carefully.

Teacher focus for activity

More able and Average: Ask questions that hint at systematic ways of working, e.g. *How did you start the problem? Why did you start there? Have you found all the possibilities? How do you know? Have you noticed any interesting patterns? Will other people be able to understand how you have recorded your solutions? Can you think of a different way of recording the solutions?*

Less able: For the boxed example on PCM 12, make sure children understand how the score of 19 has been achieved.

For problem 3, ask children to explain the method they are using to achieve each score, e.g. trying different multiples of 5 and trying to make up the difference each time with multiples of 3. Encourage children to see if they can find more than one solution for each part (**a** has 1 solution, **b** has 2 and **c** has 3).

Optional adult input

Work with the More able group. Ask questions about children's methods as suggested in the **Teacher focus for activity**.

Plenary

1 Focus on problem 1 on Textbook page 30. **Draw the '3, 5' dartboard and write '48' underneath.** Invite children to give you their solutions and to outline the methods they used. Discuss methods.

2 Involve all children in the following method, which is likely to have been used either in part or completely. Explain that the same method can be used with the other problems.

We need a score of 48 using just 3s and 5s. Where could we start? Discuss suggestions. One method is to try different multiples of 5 and to attempt to make up the difference with a multiple of 3, e.g.

$7 \times 5 = 35$

$48 - 35 = 13$, but 13 is not divisible by 3 (is not a multiple of 3) so 7 darts in the 5 ring is not a possibility.

(See **Useful mathematical information**, page 94 for information about tests of divisibility, which can help with identifying multiples.)

How could we do this systematically so that we know we have tried all possibilities? Establish that you could try the biggest multiple of 5, then the next biggest . . . until all multiples of 5 have been tried – or you could start with the smallest multiple of 5.

Draw this table with just the row headings:

number of 5s	9	8	7	6	5	4	3	2	1	0
number of 3s	1			6			11			16
winning score of 48?	✔	✗	✗	✔	✗	✗	✔	✗	✗	✔

What is the largest possible number of 5s for a score of 48? (9, since $9 \times 5 = 45$ is less than 48, but $10 \times 5 = 50$ is more than 48) Write numbers 9 to 0 in the top row of the table.

What is 9×5? (45) *How many more do we need to make 48?* (3) *Can we make this with darts in the 3 ring?* (yes: $1 \times 3 = 3$) Establish that 9 darts in the 5 ring and 1 in the 3 ring make 48. Enter the result in the first column.

Deal with the other numbers of 5s in a similar way.

Establish from the table that there are four ways of making 48. Stress that we know these are the only solutions because we have worked systematically trying all possibilities.

Discuss patterns in the table, e.g. the possible number of 5s (9, 6, 3, 0) decreases by 3 each time, while the possible number of 3s (1, 6, 11, 16) increases by 5 each time.

(For an explanation of these patterns, and of those in the solutions table for problem 2 see **Useful mathematical information**, page 95.)

Development

Children make up their own '2 number' dartboards, find a suitable 'winning score' with more than one solution and give it to a friend to solve.

Solutions

Textbook page 30

(Presentation of solutions may differ.)

1 $(9 \times 5) + (1 \times 3)$; $(6 \times 5) + (6 \times 3)$; $(1 \times 5) + (11 \times 3)$; $(0 \times 5) + (16 \times 3)$

2 $(7 \times 7) + (3 \times 3)$; $(4 \times 7) + (10 \times 3)$; $(1 \times 7) + (17 \times 3)$

PCM 12

1

darts	0	1	2	3	4	5	6	7	8	9	10	11	12
score	0	5	10	15	20	25	30	35	40	45	50	55	60

2

darts	0	1	2	3	4	5	6	7	8	9	10	11	12
score	0	3	6	9	12	15	18	21	24	27	30	33	36

3 (Presentation of solutions may differ.)

a $(2 \times 5) + (1 \times 3)$

b $(4 \times 5) + (2 \times 3)$; $(1 \times 5) + (7 \times 3)$

c $(7 \times 5) + (1 \times 3)$; $(4 \times 5) + (6 \times 3)$; $(1 \times 5) + (11 \times 3)$

24 Colourful cars

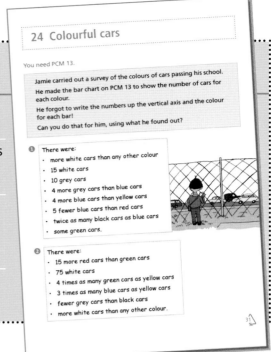

Minimum prior experience

simple bar charts with vertical axis labelled in 1s; counting on in 1s

Resources

Textbook page 31, PCM 13 with the discretionary clue removed, 2 enlarged copies of PCM 13, coloured pencils

Key vocabulary

survey, data, graph, bar chart, represent, vertical axis, label, tall, tallest

What's the problem?

Children are presented with some findings from a survey of car colours and a bar chart representing the data. The colour labels for the bars and the numbers for the graduations on the vertical axis are missing and children are asked to work out what they are. This involves reasoning about numbers, interpreting a bar chart and an understanding of scales on the vertical axis of graphs.

Problem solving objectives

● Choose and use appropriate number operations and appropriate ways of calculating to solve problems.

● Explain methods and reasoning about numbers orally and in writing.

● Use all four operations to solve word problems involving numbers in 'real life', using one or more steps.

Differentiation

All children work from Textbook page 31.

More able: problem 2.

Average: problem 2 (with discretionary clues on PCM 13).

Less able: problem 1 (same bar chart but with each interval representing 1 car and simpler data).

Introducing the problem

Allow time for children to read through the problem. Invite them to explain the context of the problem and what they are asked to do. Ensure that everyone understands that they are asked to work out the colour label for each bar and the numbering for the vertical axis.

Teacher focus for activity

All children: Encourage children to read through the clues, selecting ones that are immediately helpful, rather than trying to work through the clues in order. Ask:

● *What do you need to know first?* (the scale on the vertical axis)

● *Which clues might help you find that?* (there are more white cars than any other colour; the number of white cars)

● *How will that help you?* (by enabling you to work out what each interval represents)

● *How could you do that?* (divide the number of cars by the number of divisions on the axis)

● *What could you do next? . . .*

If children are having difficulty in working out the vertical axis scale, suggest that they estimate what it might be and try it out.

Average and Less able: If, after asking the questions suggested above, children are finding it difficult to get started, provide them with the discretionary clue from PCM 13, working through it with them if necessary.

Less able: Help children to reason about numbers and bars by asking questions such as: *If there are 6 blue cars and 4 more grey cars than blue cars, how tall will the grey bar be?*

Optional adult input

Work with the Average group, asking children to explain what they have already worked out and how they did it, and what they are currently working on and why.

Plenary

Display two large copies of PCM 13.

1 Establish the need to work out the scale of the vertical axis first. Invite children from all groups to explain how they did this:

  - For problem 1
    Reasoning from the data that, as there are more white cars than any other and that, as there are 15 white cars, the tallest bar represents 15. This bar 'measures' 15 divisions on the vertical axis, so 15 divisions represent 15 cars, and 1 division must represent 1 car.

  - For problem 2
    Establishing that the tallest bar represents 75 cars and 'measures' 15 divisions on the vertical axis, i.e. 15 divisions represent 75 cars.
    There are various ways of working out how many cars 1 division represents. Trial and improvement is probably the easiest and is likely to be the most common, e.g. estimating that each division represents 4 cars; counting up the axis in 4s; seeing that this falls short; trying 5.
    More able children may have reasoned about the numbers and calculated what each division represents. (See **Useful mathematical information,** page 95 for methods of calculation using ideas of ratio and proportion.)

  Invite children to write the numbers for the vertical axis on each copy of the bar chart.

2 Invite children to explain the steps they took to identify the labels for the bars for each problem. These will vary in order. Below is a possible route for problem 2. As the colour for each bar is identified, write it under the bar.

  - There are more white cars than any other colour, so the tallest bar (the 2nd bar) must be white.

	white					

  - There are 15 more red cars than green cars. The only two bars (excluding the white bar) with a difference of 15 (3 divisions) are the 1st and 5th. So the 1st bar (the taller) must be red and the 5th bar must be green.

red	white			green		

  - There are 4 times as many green cars as yellow cars. The green bar represents 40 cars, so the yellow bar must be $\frac{1}{4}$ of 40 = 10. The only bar representing 10 cars is the 4th, so the 4th bar must be yellow.

red	white		yellow	green		

  - There are 3 times as many blue cars as yellow cars. The yellow bar represents 10 cars so the blue bar must represent $3 \times 10 = 30$ cars. The only bar of this height is the 3rd. So the 3rd bar is blue.

red	white	blue	yellow	green		

  - There are fewer grey cars than black cars. The 6th and 7th bars are the only two left unlabelled so the 6th (the shorter) bar must be grey and the 7th bar must be black.

red	white	blue	yellow	green	grey	black

Development

Ask: *What if the number of white cars (the largest number) was 30 (45, 60, 90)?*

Solutions

For both problems, the colour labels (from left to right) are: red, white, blue, yellow, green, grey, black

Number labels from zero on the vertical axis are:

1 1, 2, 3, 4, 5, 6, 7, 8, 9, 10, 11, 12, 13, 14, 15, 16

2 5, 10, 15, 20, 25, 30, 35, 40, 45, 50, 55, 60, 65, 70, 75, 80

25 Test ramp

Minimum prior experience

adding and subtracting 2-digit multiples of 5 and 10; finding $\frac{1}{2}$ and $\frac{1}{3}$ of a simple number; familiarity with centimetres

Resources

Textbook pages 32 and 33, ramp and model car (optional)

Key vocabulary

half, third, centimetre, metre, measurement, distance

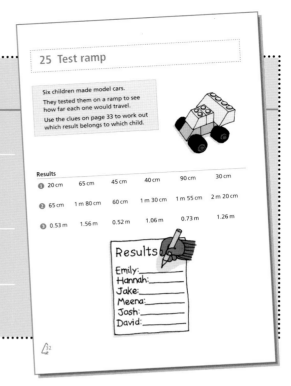

What's the problem?

Some children have used a ramp to test how far their model cars will travel. From the test results and a set of clues, children work out who each car belongs to. This involves reasoning about numbers, finding fractions and an ability to work in metres and centimetres (expressed as decimals of a metre for the more able).

Problem solving objectives

- Choose and use appropriate number operations and appropriate ways of calculating to solve problems.
- Explain methods and reasoning about numbers orally and in writing.
- Use all four operations to solve word problems involving numbers in 'real life' and measures, using one or more steps, including converting metres to centimetres and vice versa.

Differentiation

All children work from Textbook pages 32 and 33.

More able: problem 3 (decimal format for lengths).

Average: problem 2 (same problem but with different lengths, given in metres and centimetres).

Less able: problem 1 (same problem but with different lengths, given in centimetres).

Introducing the problem

Set the context of the problem: a group of children using a ramp to test how far their model cars will travel. You could use an improvised ramp and model car to demonstrate this.

Revise the number of centimetres in a metre.

Remind children that they should record what they do at each stage of the problem.

Teacher focus for activity

All children: Encourage children to read each clue carefully and to find one that will provide an 'entry' into the problem. Once one result has been worked out, ask: *Which clue could you use with this result to find another one?*

More able: Ask children how many centimetres and metres each distance represents. If children are finding it difficult to work with the distances expressed in decimals, ask them how they could make them simpler to work with (write them in centimetres). It is relatively straightforward to convert distances such as 2.45 m to centimetres, but some children may need prompting when converting 0.9 m and 1.8 m – ask, e.g. *What fraction of a metre is 0.9 m?* ($\frac{9}{10}$) *What is $\frac{1}{10}$ of a metre?* (10 cm) *What is $\frac{9}{10}$ of a metre?* (90 cm)

Average: If children find it difficult to work in metres and centimetres, ask them how they could make the distances simpler to work with (write them in centimetres).

Less able: If children are finding it difficult to get started, direct them to either of the clues involving a half.

Clues

Jake's car travelled the same distance as the total for Josh and Hannah's cars.

Meena's car travelled one third the distance that David's car travelled.

David's car travelled ½ a metre more than Emily's car.

Hannah's car travelled half the distance that Emily's car travelled.

Optional adult input

Work with the Less able group, asking questions such as: *What clue could help us? What do we know about David's result? What do we know about Emily's result? How can we decide which are David's and Emily's results?* (look for 2 results with a difference of half a metre)

Plenary

For easy reference write the clues, labelled A, B C and D.

A Jake's car travelled the same distance as the total for Josh and Hannah's cars.

B David's car travelled $\frac{1}{2}$ a metre more than Emily's car.

C Meena's car travelled one third the distance that David's car travelled.

D Hannah's car travelled half the distance that Emily's car travelled.

1 Discuss the format of the distances for each problem. Were children able to work with them as they are presented? How could (did) they make the distances simpler to work with?

Ask children to convert each distance in problems 2 and 3 to centimetres:

65 cm   180 cm   60 cm   130 cm   155 cm   220 cm
53 cm   156 cm   52 cm   106 cm   73 cm   126 cm

Ensure that children understand the process of conversion, e.g. that:

- 1 m 30 cm is the same as 100 cm + 30 cm = 130 cm;
- 1.8 m is 1 metre and $\frac{8}{10}$ of a metre. $\frac{1}{10}$ of a metre is 10 cm so $\frac{8}{10}$ of a metre is 80 cm. So 1.8 m is 1 m and 80 cm = 100 cm + 80 cm = 180 cm.

2 Tell children that you are going to focus on the second set of results. Write them on the board:

65 cm   1 m 80 cm   60 cm   1 m 30 cm 1 m 55 cm 2 m 20 cm

65cm   180 cm   60 cm   130 cm   155 cm   220 cm

Explain that, although the distances are different in each problem, the same problem solving methods can be used for each.

Invite children to suggest which clues to start with and possible routes through the problem. Establish that any clue can be used first, and that, for any starting clue, it is a matter of finding results that satisfy it.

(One route through the problem is suggested in **Useful mathematical information**, page 96.)

3 Discuss the calculations involved and the properties of numbers that children used when finding distances to satisfy a particular clue. Highlight issues such as:

- Finding two distances where one is half of the other is equivalent to finding two distances where one is double the other (clue D).
- Finding two distances where one is $\frac{1}{3}$ of the other is equivalent to finding two distances where one is three times the other (clue C).
- The relationship between finding a fraction and division, e.g. $\frac{1}{3}$ of 180 cm = 180 cm ÷ 3 = 60 cm (clue C).

Occasionally repeat a calculation using the corresponding distance from one of the other two sets of results.

Development

Children provide a different set of clues through which their problem could be solved.

Solutions

problem	Emily	Hannah	Jake	Meena	Josh	David
1	40 cm	20 cm	65 cm	30 cm	45 cm	90 cm
2	1 m 30 cm	65 cm	2 m 20 cm	60 cm	1 m 55 cm	1 m 80 cm
3	1.06 m	0.53 m	1.26 m	0.52 m	0.73 m	1.56 m

26 The Pizza Place

26 The Pizza Place

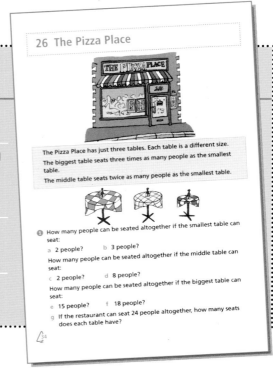

The Pizza Place has just three tables. Each table is a different size.
The biggest table seats three times as many people as the smallest table.
The middle table seats twice as many people as the smallest table.

① How many people can be seated altogether if the smallest table can seat:
   a 2 people?   b 3 people?
   How many people can be seated altogether if the middle table can seat:
   c 2 people?   d 8 people?
   How many people can be seated altogether if the biggest table can seat:
   e 15 people?   f 18 people?
   g If the restaurant can seat 24 people altogether, how many seats does each table have?

34

Minimum prior experience

multiplying and dividing numbers to 25 by 2 and 3; understanding the inverse relationship between multiplication and division

Resources

Textbook pages 34 and 35, counters

Key vocabulary

half, quarter, three quarters, third, twice as many, three times as many

What's the problem?

Children are given information about the proportion of places provided by each of three different sized tables in a pizzeria. Using further information about the number of people, children work out how many people can be seated at each of the tables. The problem involves fractions and simple ideas of proportion.

Problem solving objectives

- Choose and use appropriate number operations and appropriate ways of calculating to solve problems.
- Explain methods and reasoning about numbers orally and in writing.
- Solve mathematical problems or puzzles, recognise and explain patterns and relationships, generalise and predict. Suggest extensions by asking 'What if . . .?'

Differentiation

More able: Textbook page 35, problem 3.

Average: Textbook page 35, problem 2 (same problem but with simpler calculation).

Less able: Textbook page 34, problem 1 (series of simple problems based on the same data and context).

Introducing the problem

Allow children time to read through the introduction to the problems on Textbook page 34. Ask questions about the context to ensure that they have understood, e.g. *Where is the problem set? How many*

tables are there? What are we told about the tables? Discuss, in general terms, children's experiences of pizzerias.

Before children start, check that they understand expressions such as 'a table can seat 3 people' and '5 seats were taken'.

Teacher focus for activity

More able: If children are finding it difficult to get started, you could ask: *If $\frac{3}{4}$ of the seats are taken, what fraction are not taken?*

More able and Average: Ask children to explain how to calculate $\frac{1}{2}$ or $\frac{1}{3}$ of different numbers. Some may need reminding that if, for example, one third of a number is 8 then the whole number, which is three thirds, is $3 \times 8 = 24$. If necessary, draw shapes divided into fractions with the numbers written in.

$\frac{1}{3}$ of 24 = 8
$3 \times 8 = 24$

All children: Children may find it helpful to draw diagrams when determining the number of places at each table.

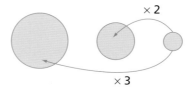

2 On Saturday night ¼ of the seats were not taken.
12 more people arrived, but there were only enough seats for ½ of them.
How many people altogether does the smallest table seat?

3 On Saturday night ¾ of the seats were taken.
18 more people arrived, but there were only enough seats for ⅓ of them.
How many people altogether does the smallest table seat?

Less able: Children may find it helpful to manipulate counters (to represent seats) between three circles (to represent tables). Prompt reasoning about numbers by asking questions such as: *If there are 2 seats at this table, how many must there be at that table, and why?*

Optional adult input

Work with the Less able group. Help children to reason about the number of places at each table, asking questions such as those suggested above and, if necessary, using counters and three circles to represent seats and tables.

Plenary

1 Focus on problem 3 on Textbook page 35. Explain that children who worked on the other problems will be able to join in because their problems are similar.

Invite children who tackled problem 3 to describe how they solved the problem.

2 Work through the following likely method, making sure that all children have an opportunity to contribute.

On Saturday night $\frac{3}{4}$ of the seats were taken so what fraction of the seats were free (not taken)? ($\frac{1}{4}$)

If necessary use different numbers of dots to represent seats to show that if $\frac{3}{4}$ of them are taken, then $\frac{1}{4}$ are free.

 $\frac{3}{4}$ (3 of the 4 rows, or 12 seats) are taken.
$\frac{1}{4}$ (1 of the 4 rows, or 4 seats) are free.

16 seats

Say: *18 people arrived. There was only room for $\frac{1}{3}$ of them. How many people was there room for?*

Discuss how $\frac{1}{3}$ of 18 can be found by dividing 18 by 3:

$\frac{1}{3}$ of 18 = 18 ÷ 3 = 6

Again, you could show this with a diagram.

Establish that there was room for 6 of the people.

 18 people divided into 3 equal rows gives 6 in each row.

So we know there were seats for 6 people and that $\frac{1}{4}$ of the seats in the restaurant were free. What does that tell us? (That $\frac{1}{4}$ of the seats in the restaurant is 6)

If $\frac{1}{4}$ of the seats is 6, how many seats are there in the restaurant?

Establish that if $\frac{1}{4}$ of the seats is 6, then all the seats (4 quarters) is 6 × 4 = 24. As before, a diagram could be use to demonstrate this.

We know that there are 24 seats in the restaurant. We know the large table seats 3 times as many people as the smallest table and the middle table seats twice as many people as the smallest table. How can we work out how many each table seats?

The most likely suggestion is trial and improvement.

Draw three circles representing the tables. Invite children, particularly from the Less able group, to suggest numbers for each table, adjusting until the proportions are right (12 at the biggest table, 8 at the middle table and 4 at the smallest).

(12)   (8)   (4)

(See **Useful mathematical information**, page 96 for an algebraic approach to this part of the solution, suitable for Year 4 children.)

Development

Ask: *What if the large table seats 4 times as many people as the smallest table and the middle table seats 3 times as many as the smallest table?*

Solutions

1 a 12 people **b** 18 people **c** 6 people
  d 24 people **e** 30 people **f** 36 people
  g 4 seats, 8 seats and 12 seats

2 4 people

3 4 people

27 Tangrams

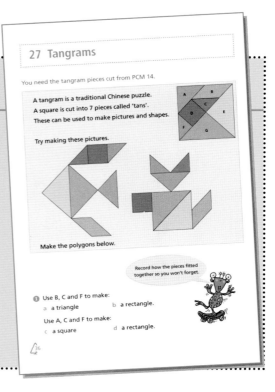

What's the problem?

Children use particular pieces from a traditional 7-piece tangram to make specified shapes. This will involve an understanding of the properties of 2-D shapes and some of the relationships between them.

Problem solving objective

● Solve mathematical problems or puzzles, recognise and explain patterns and relationships, generalise and predict. Suggest extensions by asking 'What if . . .?'

Differentiation

More able: Textbook page 37, problems 3 and 4 (using 5 and 7 tangram pieces).

Average: Textbook page 37, problems 2 and 3 (using 4 and 5 pieces).

Less able: Textbook pages 36 and 37, problems 1 and 2 (using 3 and 4 pieces).

Introducing the problem

Read through the problem introduction on Textbook page 36. Allow children a few minutes to make the pictures shown and to create some of their own.

Revise the properties of squares, rectangles, triangles, pentagons and hexagons.

Before children start their problems, remind them to sketch each solution and write on the letter labels, as it is easy to forget how a shape was constructed.

Explain that they must use all of the pieces specified for a shape, even if they could construct it with fewer.

Teacher focus for activity

All children: As children work, ask questions that focus on the properties of the shape they are trying to construct and the shapes they have to construct it with, e.g.

● *How many sides/angles does the shape have?*
● *Is there anything special about the angles/sides?* (e.g. equal, right angles)
● *What shape is this piece?*
● *How many right angles will you need for this shape?*
● *Which of these pieces have right angles?*
● *What do you get when you put 2 right angles together?* (a straight line)

Once a polygon has been constructed, can children classify it even further? (e.g. is a triangle isosceles (two equal sides), equilateral (all sides equal), right-angled or none of these?)

More able and Average: When making pentagons and hexagons, can children distinguish between those that are 'convex' (no angles greater than 2 right angles) and those that are 'concave' (1 or more angles greater than 2 right angles)? Can they make one of each?

convex pentagon

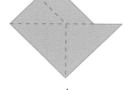

concave hexagon

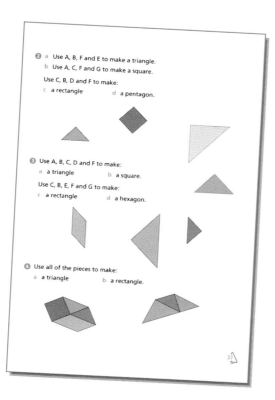

2 a Use A, B, F and E to make a triangle.
  b Use A, C, F and G to make a square.
  Use C, B, D and F to make:
  c a rectangle   d a pentagon.

3 Use A, B, C, D and F to make:
  a a triangle   b a square.
  Use C, B, E, F and G to make:
  c a rectangle   d a hexagon.

4 Use all of the pieces to make:
  a a triangle   b a rectangle.

Optional adult input

Work with the Less able group. Discuss the options for recording shapes (e.g. drawing around shapes, drawing on squared paper, sketching) and help children to choose the easiest method for them.

Plenary

Use the tangram pieces on an overhead projector or enlarged tangram pieces with Blu-Tack on the back.

1 Select, say, 2 polygons from each problem and invite children to show their solutions using the display tangram pieces. As children manipulate pieces talk about the shapes being 'rotated' and 'translated'. For each polygon constructed, discuss the tangram pieces used:

  ● their names (triangle, square, quadrilateral)

  ● their properties
    Encourage children to be specific, e.g. all the triangles are right-angled and isosceles (2 equal sides). Piece B is a parallelogram (opposite sides equal and parallel) and, although children are unlikely to be able to name it, they may be able to refer to it as a shape with equal opposite angles and sides, or as a 'slanting rectangle'.

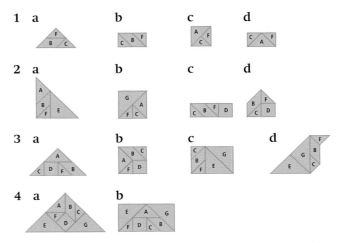

  ● properties of pieces that were helpful in making the polygon, e.g. 2 angles together making a right angle; 2 right angles making a straight line; a side of each of 2 pieces being equal to the side of the main shape.

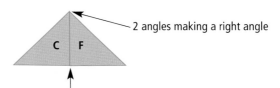

2 angles making a right angle

2 right angles making a straight line

Discuss the name and properties of the final shape. Again, encourage children to be specific and detailed, e.g. a square: is a quadrilateral; is a rectangle with 4 equal sides; has 4 right angles; is regular; is symmetrical with 4 lines of symmetry. Are the pentagons and hexagons regular or irregular? (all irregular). Are they concave or convex?

2 Invite children to explain the methods they used for recording shapes. Discuss the advantages and disadvantages of each method, e.g.

  ● **Sketching**
    This is convenient and quick, but it can be difficult sketching the shapes correctly and getting them to fit.

  ● **Drawing around shapes**
    This avoids the difficulty of sketching shapes, but can be difficult if shapes move or if they are getting 'dog-eared'. A slightly easier approach is to put a dot at each vertex of a piece and then join the dots.

  ● **Drawing on squared paper**
    At least one side of most of the pieces is an exact number of centimetres and many of the angles are right angles, which make it convenient to use squared paper.

Development

Children investigate quadrilaterals and other polygons that can be made using all 7 pieces.

Solutions

Here is one solution for each shape. There may be others.

28 Last digit patterns

28 Last digit patterns

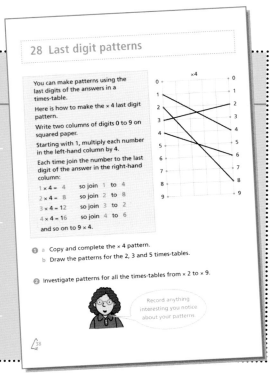

You can make patterns using the last digits of the answers in a times-table.
Here is how to make the × 4 last digit pattern.
Write two columns of digits 0 to 9 on squared paper.
Starting with 1, multiply each number in the left-hand column by 4.
Each time join the number to the last digit of the answer in the right-hand column:

1 × 4 = 4   so join 1 to 4
2 × 4 = 8   so join 2 to 8
3 × 4 = 12   so join 3 to 2
4 × 4 = 16   so join 4 to 6
and so on to 9 × 4.

1 a Copy and complete the × 4 pattern.
   b Draw the patterns for the 2, 3 and 5 times-tables.

2 Investigate patterns for all the times-tables from × 2 to × 9.

Record anything interesting you notice about your patterns.

Minimum prior experience

work out the 2, 3, 4 and 5 times-tables; draw a straight line between 2 points

Resources

Textbook page 38, PCM 15 photocopied onto an OHP transparency or enlarged for display, 1 cm squared paper, sharp pencils, rulers, multiplication tables (discretionary), small mirrors

Key vocabulary

multiple, multiply, times, digit, sequence, pattern, rule, relationship, predict, symmetry, reflect, mirror line, line of symmetry

What's the problem?

Children use the units digits of answers in multiplication tables to generate visual patterns. They investigate, describe and possibly explain and generalise about the patterns and relationships (this may involve observations about symmetry and about odd and even numbers).

Problem solving objectives

- Solve mathematical problems or puzzles, recognise and explain patterns and relationships, generalise and predict. Suggest extensions by asking 'What if . . .?'
- Make and investigate a general statement about familiar numbers or shapes by finding examples that satisfy it.

Differentiation

All children work from Textbook page 38.

More able and Average: problem 2 (investigating 2 to 9 times-tables)

Less able: problem 1 (2, 3, 4 and 5 times-tables)

Differentiation will also be by outcome.

Introducing the problem

Go over the instructions at the top of Textbook page 38 in detail. Make it clear that no line is drawn from the zero in the left-hand column (it would upset any potential symmetry). Invite children to predict which digits 5, 6 and 7 in the left-hand column of the grid

will join with (0, 4 and 8). Point out that they should put a dot by each number (at the intersections of grid lines) for lines to connect to.

Explain that making the patterns is only the start of the investigation. The most important aspect is identifying and describing patterns.

Teacher focus for activity

All children: To avoid mistakes, encourage children to work in pairs, with each child confirming the two numbers to be joined before the line is drawn. For children who are not too sure of a particular times-table, discuss how knowledge of one table can be used to generate another (see **Useful mathematical information**, pages 85–86).

Encourage children to describe any patterns and relationships they can see, e.g. in the patterns for the 2, 4, 6 and 8 times-tables, the only numbers in the right-hand column that have lines going to them are even numbers.

More able and Average: Can children identify and demonstrate any symmetry in the patterns (using small mirrors if necessary)? (e.g. in the pattern for the 7 times-table, there is symmetry about the line joining 5 to 5)

Less able: Children may need help in building up multiplication tables. Help them to do this through repeated addition or counting on. Some children may need to use a ready printed copy of the tables.

Optional adult input

Work with the More able group. Ask children to describe any patterns or relationships they can see, including symmetry.

Plenary

Display PCM 15 either as an overhead projection or enlarged on a sheet of paper. Cover up the patterns and uncover each one as it is dealt with.

Deal with each times-table in turn. For each one, invite children to show their last digit pattern and to say which digits each line joins. Ask children to check that it matches the displayed pattern. Invite children to identify patterns and relationships and discuss these. Patterns and relationships identified, and discussions, might be along the following lines:

- **2 times-table**

  All lines go to even numbers. *Why?* Establish that the result of multiplying any number by 2 (or doubling) is always even. *What would happen if the table was extended beyond 9×2?* (the same sequence of last digits would be repeated)

- **3 times-table**

  All numbers are connected except zero. *If the table was extended, what last digit would be produced next?* Lines going to the right-hand column are in clusters of 3. The pattern is symmetrical about the 5 to 5 mirror line. Invite children to point out the corresponding parts in each half.

- **4 times-table**

  All lines go to even numbers. The observation about multiplication by 2 resulting in even products could be extended to multiplication by 4: multiplying by 4 is essentially multiplying by 2 (even result) then multiplying by 2 again (even result).

- **5 times-table**

  All lines go to 0 or 5. *Why?* Discuss the effect of repeatedly adding 5, e.g. every other number (when 2 fives have been added) must be a multiple of 10 and multiples of 10 end in zero.

- **6 times-table**

  Again all lines go to an even number. The observation about multiplying by 2 and by 4 could now be extended to multiplication by any even number: multiplication by an even number results in an even number. The three sets of parallel lines are of interest. Children may need to describe them as 'going in the same direction' or 'like railway tracks'. You could introduce the term 'parallel'.

- **7 times-table**

  Children may observe that the pattern is similar to the pattern for the 3 times-table, with the clusters of 3 in the left-hand column. It is in fact a reversal (i.e. the $\times 3$ pattern flipped over).

- **8 times-table**

  This provides further evidence that multiplying by any even number results in an even number. This is a similar type of pattern to the $\times 4$ pattern with two points where several lines intersect.

- **9 times-table**

  All lines cross at the same point. The sum of the two numbers joined is always 10, so as the numbers on the left increase, the numbers they are joined to decrease. The pattern is symmetrical with 2 lines of symmetry: the 5 to 5 line and an imaginary vertical line halfway between the columns of numbers.

It is interesting to note that the only numbers whose times-tables produce patterns with symmetry ($\times 3$, $\times 5$, $\times 7$ and $\times 9$) are odd numbers. With all of them there is a 5 to 5 line. *Why?* (multiplication of an odd number by 5 results in a number ending in 5)

Development

Children investigate last digit patterns for $\times 11$, $\times 12$ and other times-tables.

Solutions

All patterns are shown on PCM 15.

Observations about each one will vary (see **Plenary**).

29 Ruritanian Lotto

Minimum prior experience

(read and) write numbers to 2000; mental addition of up to
4 single-digit numbers

Resources

Textbook page 39; spike abacuses or place value boards and counters

Key vocabulary

digit, add, sum, total, units, tens, hundreds, thousands, ten
thousands, hundred thousands, 1- (2-, 3- . . .) digit number,
systematic, order

What's the problem?

In the Ruritanian Lotto, winning numbers are those
where the sum of the digits is equal to a given
number. Children investigate what the winning
numbers are, possibly up to 6-digit numbers. The
investigation involves simple addition and reasoning
about numbers, and could involve the reading of
numbers of up to 6 digits. A successful solution
requires systematic working.

Problem solving objectives

- Explain methods and reasoning about numbers
  orally and in writing.
- Solve mathematical problems or puzzles, recognise
  and explain patterns and relationships, generalise and
  predict. Suggest extensions by asking 'What if . . .?'
- Make and investigate a general statement about
  familiar numbers or shapes by finding examples
  that satisfy it.

Differentiation

All children work from Textbook page 39.

More able: problem 3 (solutions with up to 6 digits).

Average: problem 2 (up to 5 digits).

Less able: problem 1 (up to 4 digits).

Introducing the problem

Discuss how winning numbers are decided in the
British Lotto (random drawing of numbered balls).

Explain that the investigation this lesson is about an
unusual national lottery.

Give children time to read through the problem
introduction on Textbook page 39. Ask questions to
determine whether children have understood, e.g.
*How are winning numbers decided? Tell me a number you
could not choose.* (Any number with a zero digit)

Invite children to give you some winning numbers if
the winning digit sum was 7 (e.g. 232, 1222). Before
they start, remind them that they are being asked to
find all possible winning numbers.

Teacher focus for activity

More able and Average: Ask children to explain how
they are tackling the investigation. Encourage
children who are working fairly randomly to work
systematically, by asking questions such as:

- *How will you know when you have found all the winning
  numbers?*
- *How will you know that you haven't missed any winning
  numbers? Can you think of a way of working so that you
  won't miss any winning numbers?*
- *What is the smallest winning number? And the next?
  What is the biggest winning number?*

Less able: Children may find it helpful to use a spike
abacus or a place value board and counters. They
could manipulate 2 (3 or 4) beads or counters
representing the sum of the digits between the places
or spikes, recording each different number that
results. Encourage them to do this systematically,

perhaps starting with all beads/counters in the units, then gradually transferring them to the tens, then the hundreds . . .

winning digit sum: 4

13

Optional adult input

Work with the Less able group, helping children as described above.

Plenary

1 Discuss results for each winning digit sum from 2 to 4 in turn, starting with 2.

- **Winning sum 2**
  Invite the Less able group to give the winning numbers. Establish that there are only 2 possible winning numbers: 2 and 11.

- **Winning sum 3**
  Again, invite the Less able group to give their solutions. Establish that there are 4 possible winning numbers: 3, 12, 21 and 111.

- **Winning sum 4**
  What are the smallest and largest numbers? (4 and 1111) *How do you know?* Establish that the only single-digit number possible is 4, so it must be the smallest number. The largest number of digits possible is 4 (1, 1, 1 and 1) so 1111 must be the largest number.

Elicit that from now on the number of winning numbers is likely to increase, so, to ensure that no numbers are missed, some sort of system needs to be established. (See **Useful mathematical information**, page 85 on the importance of systematic working.) Discuss possible systematic methods. Ask children to generate the winning numbers using one of the systems and write them on the board. These might include:

a Finding all the 1-, then 2-, then 3-, then 4-digit numbers.
  Within each category there could be a further sub-system, e.g. dealing with numbers beginning with 1 first, then 2 . . . This system automatically produces a list ordered by size:

4
13   22   31
112 121 211
1111

b Finding all the numbers beginning with 1, then 2, then 3, then 4.

Again, a further sub-system could be employed within each category, e.g in the '1' category, listing all numbers starting with 4 ones, then 3 ones . . .

1111   112   121   13
211   22
31
4

Point out that whichever system is used, the largest and smallest numbers appear at each end of the list.

2 Review how many winning numbers there are for digit sums of 2, 3 and 4. Establish that the numbers of winning numbers so far have been 2, 4 and 8. (You could include 1 as the only winning number for a digit sum of 1, giving the series: 1, 2, 4 and 8.) Ask children to predict how many winning numbers there will be for a digit sum of 5. Elicit that, because in the series 1, 2, 4, 8 each number is double the previous number, 16 could be a prediction.

3 Use one of the systematic methods to establish the winning numbers for a digit sum of 5. These are (set out using system **a** above):

5
14   23   32   41
113   122   131   212   221   311
1112 1121 1211 2111
11111

Establish that there are indeed 16 numbers.

Ask children to predict how many winning numbers there would be for a digit sum of 6 (using the doubling pattern, this would be 32). If there is time, establish the winning numbers as before. Establish that there are 32 numbers (see solution for problem 3).

Development

Children investigate winning numbers with a digit sum of 7, first predicting how many there will be. (64)

Solutions

1 a 2, 11   **b** 3, 12, 21, 111   **c** 4, 13, 22, 31, 112, 121, 211, 1111

2 5, 14, 23, 32, 41, 113, 122, 131, 212, 221, 311, 1112, 1121, 1211, 2111, 11111

3 6, 15, 24, 33, 42, 51, 114, 123, 132, 141, 213, 222, 231, 312, 321, 411, 1113, 1122, 1131, 1212, 1221, 1311, 2112, 2121, 2211, 3111, 11112, 11121, 11211, 12111, 21111, 111111

30 Cutting the cake

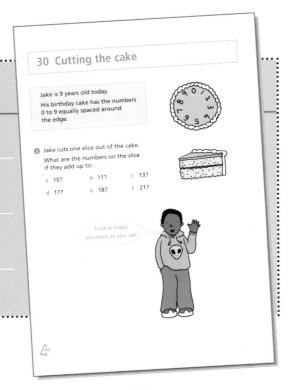

30 Cutting the cake

Jake is 9 years old today.
His birthday cake has the numbers
0 to 9 equally spaced around
the edge.

① Jake cuts one slice out of the cake.
What are the numbers on the slice
if they add up to:

a 10?   b 11?   c 13?

d 17?   e 18?   f 21?

Find as many
solutions as you can.

Minimum prior experience

adding 2 or more single-digit numbers

Resources

Textbook pages 40 and 41, PCM 16, enlarged copy of PCM 16

Key vocabulary

add, sum, total, divide, fraction, tenth

What's the problem?

A circular birthday cake has numbers 0 to 9 equally spaced around the circumference. Children use information about the sums of numbers on slices to identify how they are cut. The problem involves mental addition of 2 or more single-digit numbers and reasoning about numbers, and may involve finding fractions of a whole and an understanding of tenths and equivalent fractions.

Problem solving objectives

● Choose and use appropriate number operations and appropriate ways of calculating to solve problems.

● Explain methods and reasoning about numbers orally and in writing.

● Solve mathematical problems or puzzles, recognise and explain patterns and relationships, generalise and predict. Suggest extensions by asking 'What if . . .?'

Differentiation

More able: Textbook page 41, problem 3 (a problem involving fractions).

Average: Textbook page 41, problems 2 (similar problem but with no fractions).

Less able: Textbook page 40, problem 1 (similar but easier problems).

Introducing the problem

Read through the problem introduction on Textbook page 40.

Ensure children understand that the cake is circular and that a 'slice' involves 2 cuts from the centre of the cake to the circumference. A slice can be of any size – draw a diagram to illustrate a slice with an angle greater than 2 right angles.

Ask a few questions involving one slice, e.g. *If the total of the numbers on a slice is 3, what could the numbers be?* (0, 1 and 2; 1 and 2; 3) *What if the total is 5?* (2 and 3; 5)

Teacher focus for activity

More able: Ask children to explain their strategies. For **3a**, children may use trial and improvement methods. There is a more direct method that you could hint at by asking children to estimate the total on each slice (see **Plenary**, part 3). Ensure children understand that the whole cake is cut into three.

If children are having difficulty with **3b**, ask: *What if there was only one number on the slice, what fraction of the cake would the slice be?*

Average: For children working in a fairly random way, ask: *Can you think of a more organised way of working that ensures you find all the possibilities?*

Less able: Encourage children to be systematic, trialling consecutive pairs, 3s . . . in order around the cake.

Optional adult input

Work with the Less able group. Ask children to explain how they are working out the numbers on each slice.

Plenary

Display a large copy of PCM 16.

1 Ask the Less able group to give you their answers for problem 1, referring to the display 'cakes' each time. Encourage children to offer more than one solution where possible.

Discuss methods. These may include random trials and systematic working (e.g. adding consecutive numbers in order starting with pairs, then 3s . . .).

2 Invite the Average group to explain their methods for problem 2. These are likely to range from random trials to more systematic investigations, e.g. investigating possible pairs of slices with a total of 1, then 2, then 3 . . . Remind children that no two slices can include the same number.

Invite children to give you pairs of slices with equal totals in a systematic way and record them on the board. Establish that working systematically makes it less likely that possibilities will be missed. (See **Useful mathematical information**, page 85 on the importance of working systematically.)

3 Invite the More able group to give the solution to problem **3a** and to explain their methods. These will probably involve random or systematic trials. However, some may have totalled all the cake numbers (45), reasoned that the total on each slice must be 45 ÷ 3 = 15, then found three sets of

numbers each with a total of 15. If this is not a method used, elicit it, starting with: *What would you estimate the total on each slice to be?* Once the first set is found, the other two sets follow on, so, e.g. if (7, 8) is discovered first, then (9, 0, 1, 2, 3) is the next set and (4, 5, 6) is the third.

Another method (linking with problem **2**) would be to find all possible slices with a total of 15, then to look for three slices that include all the numbers from 0 to 9.

Draw the slices on one of the display cakes.

4 Ask children to give the fraction of the whole cake that each slice is and to explain their reasoning.

The most likely method is to reason that, because there are 10 numbers, if there was 1 number on each slice, the slice would be $\frac{1}{10}$ of the whole cake so:

- a slice with 2 numbers is $\frac{2}{10}$;
- a slice with 3 numbers is $\frac{3}{10}$;
- a slice with 5 numbers is $\frac{5}{10}$.

Children may recognise that $\frac{2}{10}$ is equivalent to $\frac{1}{5}$ and $\frac{5}{10}$ is equivalent to $\frac{1}{2}$. (See **Useful mathematical information**, page 96 on using fraction walls to demonstrate equivalent fractions.)

Development

The cake is cut into 3 slices. The sum of the numbers on 2 slices are equal, and double that of the numbers on the third slice. What are the numbers on each slice?

Solutions

1 **a** (9, 0, 1); (1, 2, 3, 4); (0, 1, 2, 3, 4)
   b (5, 6)
   c (6, 7)
   d (8, 9); (8, 9, 0)
   e (5, 6, 7); (3, 4, 5, 6)
   f (6, 7, 8); (1, 2, 3, 4, 5, 6); (0, 1, 2, 3, 4, 5, 6)

2 (The sum of the numbers on each slice is given as well as the numbers themselves)
   3: (0, 1, 2) and (3); (1, 2) and (3)
   5: (2, 3) and (5)
   6: (0, 1, 2, 3) and (6); (1, 2, 3) and (6)
   7: (3, 4) and (7)
   9: (2, 3, 4) and (9); (2, 3, 4) and (9, 0); (4, 5) and (9);
      (4, 5) and (9, 0)
   12: (3, 4, 5) and (9, 0, 1, 2)
   15: (0, 1, 2, 3, 4, 5) and (7, 8); (1, 2, 3, 4, 5) and (7, 8);
      (4, 5, 6) and (7, 8); (4, 5, 6) and (9, 0, 1, 2, 3);
      (7, 8) and (9, 0, 1, 2, 3)

3 **a** (7, 8), (4, 5, 6) and (9, 0, 1, 2, 3)
   b $\frac{2}{10}$ or $\frac{1}{5}$; $\frac{3}{10}$; $\frac{5}{10}$ or $\frac{1}{2}$

Useful mathematical information

These pages provide further explanation of the mathematics used in some lessons. Each section is referenced to the relevant activity so that it is easy to find what is needed starting from the lesson plan for the problem.

Some sections cover the mathematics that underpins the problem. Other sections cover specific mathematical concepts that children will need to understand. Both are intended to be information for the non-specialist mathematics teacher.

Possible approaches to What are we?

(Lesson 1)

Here is a method of solution for each of the problems in Lesson 1, except for problem 4, which was dealt with in the **Plenary**.

- **Problem 1**

  The number has two digits that are both different and have a sum of 9. Possibilities for digits are therefore 0 and 9, 1 and 8, 2 and 7, 3 and 6, and 4 and 5.

  The difference between the digits is 3, so possibilities are reduced to 3 and 6.

  The units digit is half the tens digit so the number is **63**.

- **Problem 2**

  The number has three digits that are all different.

  The units digit is an odd number less than 6, i.e. 1, 3 or 5.

  Possibilities for the number so far are:

  ☐ ☐ 1, ☐ ☐ 3 and ☐ ☐ 5

  The tens digit is 6 more than the units digit:

  $1 + 6 = 7$

  $3 + 6 = 9$

  However $5 + 6 = 11$, so this can be discarded as a possibility.

  Possibilities are now:

  ☐ 7 1 and ☐ 9 3

The final clue tells us that the hundreds digit is the result of adding the units and tens digits:

$7 + 1 = 8$

However $9 + 3 = 12$, so that can be discarded.

The one possibility remaining is **871**.

- **Problem 3**

  The number has three digits that are all different.

  The tens digit is double the units digit, so the possibilities for the numbers are:

  ☐ 8 4, ☐ 6 3, ☐ 4 2, ☐ 2 1 and ☐ 0 0

  The third clue tells us that the units digit is odd, so the possibilities are reduced to:

  ☐ 6 3 and ☐ 2 1

  The final clue tells us that the sum of the digits is 14:

  For the first possibility above, 5 needs to be added to 6 and 3 to make 14, giving a result of 563.

  For the second possibility above, 11 would need to be added to 2 and 1 to make 14, so this can be discarded.

  So the solution is **563**.

- **Problem 5**

  The number has four digits that are all different.

  The second clue tells us that the units digit is one third of the thousands digit which gives the following possibilities:

  9 ☐ ☐ 3, 6 ☐ ☐ 2 and 3 ☐ ☐ 1

  The second clue also tells us that the units digit is 3 less than the hundreds digit. So the possibilities are now:

  9 6 ☐ 3, 6 5 ☐ 2 and 3 4 ☐ 1

  The final clue tells us that the tens digit is 1 added to half the hundreds digit:

  In the first possibility above, half of 6 add 1 is 4 giving us 9643.

  In the second possibility, the result is $3\frac{1}{2}$, which is clearly not a digit and so can be discarded.

  In the third possibility, the result is 3, but there is already a 3 in the thousands place, so this possibility can be discarded.

  The number must be **9643**.

● **Problem 6**

The number has 5 digits that are all different.

The units digit is double the ten thousands digit. This produces the following possibilities:

1 □ □ □ 2, 2 □ □ □ 4, 3 □ □ □ 6 and 4 □ □ □ 8

(Zero for the ten thousands digit can be discounted because whole numbers do not normally begin with zero.)

However, the final clue tells us that the ten thousands digit is even, which reduces the possibilities to:

2 □ □ □ 4 and 4 □ □ □ 8

The units digit is 1 less than the tens digit, giving us these possibilities:

2 □ □ 5 4 and 4 □ □ 9 8

The thousands digit is the difference between the tens and the ten thousands digits, giving us possibilities of:

2 3 □ 5 4 and 4 5 □ 9 8

The hundreds digit is the sum of the ten thousands digit and the units digit:

In the first possibility above, this results in 23 654.

In the second possibility the result is 12, which is not a digit and so can be discarded.

The solution must be **23 654**.

What if the ten thousands digit is odd?

If the ten thousands digit was odd the two possibilities after the first 'filter' would be:

1 □ □ □ 2 and 3 □ □ □ 6

then, after the second 'filter':

1 □ □ 3 2 and 3 □ □ 7 6

Finding the difference between the tens and ten thousands digit results in possibilities of 1 2 □ 3 2 and 3 4 □ 7 6. In the first possibility there are two 2s, so that can be discarded, leaving 3 4 □ 7 6.

Finally, adding the ten thousands and units digits gives the final solution of **34 976**.

Using systematic working to find combinations

(Lessons 2, 14, 18, 29 and 30)

The solution to many problems in mathematics involves finding all possible combinations of items. This is a branch of mathematics called combinatorial analysis or combinatorics, and can often be used as an alternative to using algebra to solve a problem.

Working in a systematic ordered way is an essential part of the process. It would be worthwhile giving children problems which provide practice at this, e.g.

● *In a lucky dip game you take 3 coloured balls from a bag. If all the balls are the same colour you win a prize. If the balls in the bag are red, yellow and blue, what are the possible combinations of colours you could pull out?*

One way of tackling this is to find all the possible combinations that include red, then all the remaining combinations that include yellow, and then the remaining combination of all blues:

RRR, RRY, RRB, RYY, RYB, RBB, YYY, YYB, YBB, BBB

● *What are all the possible 3-digit numbers that can be made using the digits 1, 2 and 3?*

One way of tackling this is to find all the numbers beginning with 1, then all those beginning with 2, and then all those beginning with 3:

111, 112, 113, 121, 122, 123, 131, 132, 133, 211, 212, 213, 221, 222, 223, 231, 232, 233, 311, 312, 313, 321, 322, 323, 331, 332, 333

Other contexts that can be used are possible combinations of colours on a flag, clothes to dress in, foods from a menu or partners from a group of children.

The relationships between times-tables

(Lessons 3, 6, 7 and 28)

If the 4 and 8 times-tables are not known, they can be derived from the 2 times-table:

● **4 times-table**

Because 4 is double 2, facts from the 4 times-table can be derived by doubling facts from the 2 times-table, e.g.

$5 \times 2 = 10$, so $5 \times 4 = $ double $10 = 20$

$7 \times 2 = 14$, so $7 \times 4 = $ double $14 = 28$

● **8 times-table**

Because 8 is double 4, facts from the 8 times-table can be derived by doubling facts from the 4 times-table, e.g.

$6 \times 4 = 24$, so $6 \times 8 = $ double $24 = 48$

$9 \times 4 = 36$, so $9 \times 8 = $ double $36 = 72$

Facts from the 8 times-table can also be derived directly from the 2 times-table by doubling and doubling again, e.g.

3 × 2 = 6,
so 3 × 8 = double 6 doubled = 12 doubled = 24

8 × 2 = 16,
so 8 × 8 = double 16 doubled = 32 doubled = 64

There are similar 'double' relationships between the 3 and 6 times-tables.

Relating 'Money bags' to the binary numeration system

(Lesson 4)

(It is not expected that children should understand this.)

Our numeration system is a base 10 place value system.
When we have 10 in any column, we exchange it for 1 of the next larger unit (we exchange 10 units for 1 ten, 10 tens for 1 hundred . . .) So, moving from right to left, the value of each successive place in a number increases tenfold:
1, 10, 100, 1000, 10 000 . . .
Moving from left to right, the value of each successive place decreases ten times.

1000s	100s	10s	1s

In the binary or base 2 numeration system, we exchange every time we have 2 in any column (we exchange 2 units for a two, 2 twos for a four, 2 fours for an eight . . .) So, moving from right to left in a numeral, the value of each successive place increases twofold (is doubled): 1, 2, 4, 8, 16, 32 . . . Moving from right to left, the value of each successive place decreases two times (is halved). So the place value headings are:

16s	8s	4s	2s	1s

The largest digit that can appear in the base ten system of numeration is 9. In the binary system it is 1 – the digit in each place is either 0 or 1. Any number can be represented in the binary system, e.g. 6 in base ten is represented as 110 in binary (1 × 4, 1 × 2 and 0 × 1):

16s	8s	4s	2s	1s
		1	1	0

21 in base ten is represented as 10101 (1 × 16, 0 × 8, 1 × 4, 0 × 2 and 1 × 1);

16s	8s	4s	2s	1s
1	0	1	0	1

It follows that if we have bags of money containing 1p, 2p, 4p, 8p, 16p . . . any amount of money can be paid (up to the maximum possible amount) using single bags, e.g. 30 can be represented in binary as 11110:

16s	8s	4s	2s	1s
1	1	1	1	0

so 30p can be paid using 4 bags containing 16p, 8p, 4p and 2p.

Commutative, associative and distributive laws

(Lesson 6)

According to The National Numeracy Strategy *Framework for teaching mathematics*, 'pupils do not need to know the names of these laws but you need to discuss the ideas thoroughly since they underpin strategies for calculation and, later on, algebraic ideas'.

● **The commutative law**

   Addition and multiplication are said to be commutative because swapping the numbers around makes no difference to the answer (think of numbers **commuting** from one place to another), e.g.

$$6 + 3 = 3 + 6 = 9$$
$$4 \times 5 = 5 \times 4 = 20$$

   Commutativity can be generalised as:

$$a + b = b + a \qquad a \times b = b \times a$$

   Subtraction and division are not commutative:

$$a - b \neq b - a \qquad a \div b \neq b \div a$$

● **The associative law**

   Addition and multiplication are said to be associative because the way in which we group numbers when adding or multiplying does not matter (think of numbers forming different **associations**). Take, for example, 7 + 9 + 4:

   It makes no difference to the answer if we add the first two numbers and then add the third:

$$(7 + 9) + 4 = 16 + 4 = 20$$

   or if we add the last two numbers and then add the total to the first number:

$$7 + (9 + 4) = 7 + 13 = 20$$

Consider $2 \times 3 \times 4$:

It makes no difference to the answer whether we multiply the 2 and the 3 first and multiply the result by 4:

$$(2 \times 3) \times 4 = 6 \times 4 = 24$$

or if we multiply 3 by 4 first and then multiply 2 by the product:

$$2 \times (3 \times 4) = 2 \times 12 = 24$$

Associativity can be generalised as:

$$a + (b + c) = (a + b) + c$$
$$a \times (b \times c) = (a \times b) \times c$$

Subtraction and division are not associative:

$$a - (b - c) \neq (a - b) - c$$
$$a \div (b \div c) \neq (a \div b) \div c$$

- **The distributive law**

Multiplication is said to be distributive over addition. At its simplest, this means that when you multiply two numbers, you can represent one of the numbers as an addition and multiply each number in the addition separately, then add the results. Take, for example, 3×65. A common mental strategy would be to split up (think of **distribute**) the 65 into 60 and 5, then work out 3×60 (= 180), then 3×5 (= 15) and add the two results (180 + 15 = 195). The whole process can be shown as:

$$3 \times 65 = 3 \times (60 + 5) = (3 \times 60) + (3 \times 5)$$
$$= 180 + 15 = 195$$

This doesn't only work when we split a number into tens and units, e.g. we could split 65 into 50 and 15 instead:

$$3 \times 65 = 3 \times (50 + 15) = (3 \times 50) + (3 \times 15)$$
$$= 150 + 45 = 195$$

Multiplication is also distributive over subtraction. In other words we can express one of the numbers in a multiplication as a subtraction, multiply each of the numbers in the subtraction separately and then subtract the results. Take 5×49, for example:

$$5 \times 49 = 5 \times (50 - 1) = (5 \times 50) - (5 \times 1)$$
$$= 250 - 5 = 245$$

We can generalise the distributivity of multiplication over addition and subtraction like this:

$$a \times (b + c) = (a \times b) + (a \times c)$$
$$a \times (b - c) = (a \times b) - (a \times c)$$

Shape mobiles: an alternative solution

(Lesson 7)

Here is an alternative method for solving Textbook page 10, problem 2 (a similar method can be used with problems 1 and 3).

List all the multiples of 5 below 52:
5 10 15 20 25 30 35 40 45 50
List all the multiples of 6 below 52:
6 12 18 24 30 36 42 48

Complete this table, which shows every multiple of 5 below 52 added to every multiple of 6 below 52. Sums greater than 52 (the total number of straws) need not be entered.

+	5	10	15	20	25	30	35	40	45	50
6	11	16	21	26	31	36	41	46	51	
12	17	22	27	32	37	42	47	52		
18	23	28	33	38	43	48				
24	29	34	39	44	49					
30	35	40	45	50						
36	41	46	51							
42	47	52								
48										

It can be seen that 52 occurs twice:

- where 12 (2×6) has been added to 40 (8×5), representing 2 hexagons and 8 pentagons;
- where 42 (7×6) has been added to 10 (2×5), representing 7 hexagons and 2 pentagons.

So 52 straws can be used in making 2 hexagons and 8 pentagons or 7 hexagons and 2 pentagons with no remaining straws.

Number line race: tables of workings for the Textbook problems

(Lesson 8)

- **Problem 1**

	start	1	2	3	4	5	6	7	8	9	10	11	12	13	14	15	16	17	18	19	20
														jumps							
Fred	8	11	14	17	20	23	26	29	32	35	38	42	44	47	50						
Freda	−30	−26	−22	−18	−14	−10	−6	−2	2	6	10	14	18	22	26	30	34	38	42	46	50
Francis	−46	−40	−34	−28	−22	−16	−10	−4	2	8	14	20	26	32	38	44	50				

Fred reaches 50 first in 14 jumps.

Freda and Francis are 6 jumps and 2 jumps behind him, respectively.

- **Problem 2**

	start	1	2	3	4	5	6	7	8	9	10	11	12	13	14	15	16	17	18
														jumps					
Fred	4	10	16	33	28	34	40	46	52	58	64	70	76	82	88	94	100		
Freda	−26	−17	−8	1	10	19	28	37	46	55	64	73	82	91	100				
Francis	−98	−87	−76	−65	−54	−43	−32	−21	−10	1	12	23	34	45	56	67	78	89	100

Freda reaches 100 first in 14 jumps.

Fred and Francis are 2 jumps and 4 jumps behind her, respectively.

Number line race: an alternative method

(Lesson 8)

You could discuss the following method for problem 2 on Textbook page 11, with the More able group:

- **Deal with Fred's jumps**

  Fred jumps from 4 to 100 in equal jumps of 6.

  The difference between 4 and 100 is 96. So Fred jumps 96 in equal jumps of 6.

  To find out how many jumps he makes in getting from 4 to 100 we need to find out how many 6s there are in 96. In other words, we need to divide 96 by 6: $96 \div 6$.

  Discuss ways in which this could be done. A subtraction method could be used, either mentally with jottings or in a standard format where multiples of the divisor are subtracted from 96:

  $$
  \begin{array}{r}
  96 \\
  -\ 60 \quad (10 \times 6) \\
  \hline
  36 \\
  -\ 36 \quad (6 \times 6) \\
  \hline
  0
  \end{array}
  $$

  So there are $10 + 6 = 16$ sixes in 96.

  So Fred reaches 96 in 16 jumps.

- **Deal with Freda's jumps**

  Freda jumps from −26 to 100 in equal jumps of 9.

  The difference between −26 and 100 is slightly more difficult to calculate. One method is to count on from −26 to 0 (26), then count on from 0 to 100 (100) and add the two results (126).

  So Freda jumps 126 in jumps of 9.

  To find out how many jumps she makes in getting from −26 to 100, we need to find out how many 9s there are in 126. In other words, we need to divide 126 by 9: $126 \div 9$.

  Using the subtraction method, we find that $126 \div 9 = 14$.

  $$
  \begin{array}{r}
  126 \\
  -\ 90 \quad (10 \times 9) \\
  \hline
  36 \\
  -\ 36 \quad (4 \times 9) \\
  \hline
  0
  \end{array}
  $$
  So, $126 \div 9 = 14$

  So Freda reaches 100 in 14 jumps.

- **Deal with Francis's jumps**

  Francis jumps from −98 to 100 in equal jumps of 11.

  The difference between −98 and 0 is 98. The difference between 0 and 100 is 100. So the difference between −98 and 100 is 198.

So Francis jumps 198 in jumps of 11.

To find out how many jumps he makes in getting from −98 to 100, we need to find out how many 11s there are in 198. In other words, we need to divide 198 by 11: 198 ÷ 11.

Using the subtraction method, we find that 198 ÷ 11 = 18.

```
   198
 − 110   (10 × 11)
    88
 −  88   (8 × 11)
     0
 198 ÷ 11 = 18
```

So Francis reaches 100 in 18 jumps.

● **Compare the results for each frog**

Freda arrives at 100 first in 14 jumps.

Fred is 2 jumps behind (16 jumps) and Francis is 4 jumps behind (18 jumps).

Finding non-unit fractions of numbers

(Lesson 9)

The function of the denominator

The bottom numeral in a fraction is the denominator. It represents the number of equal parts a number has been divided into (what the number has been divided by).

$$\frac{1}{5} \longleftarrow \text{denominator}$$

So $\frac{1}{5}$ of 35 can be found by dividing 35 by 5:

$\frac{1}{5}$ of 35 = 35 ÷ 5 = 7

$\frac{1}{3}$ of 15 can be found by dividing 15 by 3:

$\frac{1}{3}$ of 15 = 15 ÷ 3 = 5

The function of the numerator

The upper numeral in a fraction is the numerator. It represents the number of those equal parts that the denominator has divided a number into.

$$\frac{2}{5} \longleftarrow \text{numerator}$$

For example, since $\frac{1}{5}$ of 35 is 7 (see above), then $\frac{2}{5}$ of 35 is 2 × 7 = 14.

Emphasising the verbal representation of fractions will help children to understand this:

If **one** fifth of 35 is 7 then **two** fifths must be **2 × 7**; **three** fifths must be **3 × 7 = 21**; **four** fifths must be **4 × 7 = 28**; **five** fifths must be **5 × 7 = 35**.

Fair shares: solutions

(Lesson 9)

Here are tables providing the solutions for the problem on Textbook page 12 and Fair shares 2 on PCM 4 (the solution table for Fair shares 1 on PCM 4 is given in the **Plenary** to the lesson):

● **Textbook page 12**

starting numbers		finishing numbers	
Amy	Ben	Amy (− 2)	Ben (+ 2)
2	1	0	3
4	2	2	4
6	3	4	5
8	4	6	6

Amy starts with 8 sweets and Ben starts with 4 sweets.

● **PCM 4, Fair shares 2**

starting numbers		finishing numbers	
Amy	Ben	Amy (− 6)	Ben (+ 6)
6	4	0	10
9	6	3	12
12	8	6	14
15	10	9	16
18	12	12	18
21	14	15	20
24	16	18	22
27	18	21	24
30	20	24	26
33	22	27	28
36	24	30	30

Amy starts with 36 sweets and Ben starts with 24 sweets.

Puzzling symbols: calculations for problems 1 and 3

(Lesson 10)

Here are the most likely steps for problems 1 and 3 on Textbook page 13, together with the calculations involved.

- ### Step 1: 3rd column

  Find the value of the ✳ by dividing the column total by 4.

  1   $8 \div 4 = 2$

  So, ✳ = 2

  3   $72 \div 4 = 18$

  So, ✳ = 18

- ### Step 2: 2nd row

  Subtract the sum of the two ✳ values from the total to give the sum of the two ◆s. Dividing the sum of the ◆s by 2 will give the value of one ◆.

  1   $14 - (2 + 2) = 14 - 4 = 10$

  $10 \div 2 = 5$

  So, ◆ = 5

  3   $78 - (18 + 18) = 78 - 36 = 42$

  $42 \div 2 = 21$

  So, ◆ = 21

- ### Step 3: 2nd column

  Subtract the values of the ◆ and ✳ from the column total to give the sum of the two ⊙s.

  Divide the sum of the two ⊙s by 2 to give the value of one ⊙.

  1   $13 - (5 + 2) = 13 - 7 = 6$

  $6 \div 2 = 3$

  So, ⊙ = 3

  3   $77 - (21 + 18) = 77 - 39 = 38$

  $38 \div 2 = 19$

  So, ⊙ = 19

- ### Step 4

  Find all the missing totals by adding numbers in rows and columns.

  1

5	3	2	3	13
2	5	2	5	14
5	3	2	5	15
3	2	2	3	10
15	13	8	16	

  3

21	19	18	19	77
18	21	18	21	78
21	19	18	21	79
19	18	18	19	74
79	77	72	80	

Palindromic investigation: sums of digits

(Lesson 13)

It is interesting to note that the sums of the digits of 2-digit numbers are peculiar to the number of addition stages in which they produce palindromic numbers.

The sum of the digits of:

- all 1-stage numbers is 2, 3, 4, 5, 6, 7, 8, 9 or 11;
- all 2-stage numbers is 10, 12 or 13;
- all 3-stage numbers is 14;
- all 4-stage numbers is 15;
- all 6-stage numbers is 16;
- the 24-stage number is 17.

Windows: a systematic method

(Lesson 14)

Here is an example of a systematic method for solving problem 1 on Textbook page 18. A similar approach can be applied to problem 2.

There are 6 red squares and no 3 red squares in a line are allowed.

Since there are 3 rows and 3 columns, there must be exactly 2 red squares in each, because:

- More than 2 red squares is not allowed.
- Fewer than 2 red squares in a row or column would result in one or more rows or columns having more than 2 red squares (to make up the total 6), which is not allowed.

We can now start off our systematic approach by fixing 2 red squares together in the left of the top row and investigating possible arrangements in the 2nd and 3rd rows without creating 3 in a line:

1   No red squares can be added in the 3rd row without forming 3 in a line.

2

3 One more red square can be added in the 3rd row (to the bottom left) but another red square in the bottom row would form 3 in a line.

Clearly, arrangement **2** is a solution.

Now we can fix 2 red squares in the first and last squares of the top row:

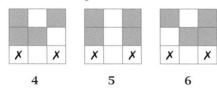

Arrangements **4**, **5** and **6** produce no solutions (adding 2 red squares to the 3rd row would result in 3 red squares in a line).

Now we can fix 2 red squares in the right of the top row:

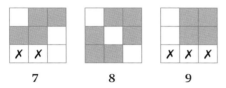

For arrangements **7** and **9**, adding 2 red squares to the 3rd row would result in 3 red squares in a line.

Clearly, arrangement **8** is a solution.

All possible arrangements have now been investigated. Arrangements **2** and **8** are the solutions, but as one can be transformed into the other by rotating or turning the window over, they are essentially the same window.

(See below for more about rotations.)

Are rotated or reflected shapes the same?

(Lessons 14 and 17)

These shapes are the same – they are just rotations of each another. The second shape is the first shape rotated through one right angle clockwise. Children can demonstrate this for themselves by tracing one of the shapes and rotating and sliding (translating) the traced shape so that it fits over the other shape.

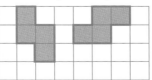

These shapes are reflections of each other. Children can show this by putting a mirror between them along the dotted line. Whether 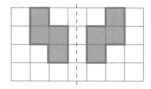 they are considered as different shapes will depend upon the context. When we are considering plane shapes or patterns drawn on paper, as in Lesson 17, reflections can be considered as different shapes – we cannot fit one on top of the other by sliding (translating) or rotating, we could only do this by flipping them over. However, when dealing with shapes in a 3-D context such as the windows in Lesson 14, reflected shapes or patterns can be considered to be the same, because within that context they can be flipped over.

These shapes are reflections. However, they are also rotations and, because one could be rotated and slid on top of the other, they are mathematically the same shape.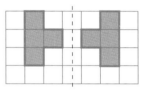

Shapes that are the same shape and size are described in mathematics as being **congruent**. This term is introduced in Year 5 of the *Framework for teaching mathematics*.

Shapes that are reflections of one another, but are the same shape and size in every other respect, are said to have '**indirect congruence**'.

Number neighbours: results table and observations

(Lesson 15)

This table shows all the sums of 2, 3, 4 . . . consecutive numbers with totals up to 40 (they exclude zero).

sum	number of consecutive numbers						
	2	3	4	5	6	7	8
1							
2							
3	1,2						
4							
5	2,3						
6		1,2,3					
7	3,4						
8							
9	4,5	2,3,4					
10			1,2,3,4				
11	5,6						
12		3,4,5					
13	6,7						
14			2,3,4,5				
15	7,8	4,5,6		1,2,3,4,5			
16							
17	8,9						
18		5, 6, 7	3,4,5,6				
19	9,10						
20				2,3,4,5,6			
21	10,11	6,7,8			1,2,3,4,5,6		
22			4,5,6,7				
23	11,12						
24		7,8,9					
25	12,13			3,4,5,6,7			
26			5,6,7,8				
27	13,14	8,9,10			2,3,4,5,6,7		
28						1,2,3,4,5,6,7	
29	14,15						
30		9,10,11	6,7,8,9	4,5,6,7,8			
31	15,16						
32							
33	16,17	10,11,12			3,4,5,6,7,8		
34			7,8,9,10				
35	17,18			5,6,7,8,9		2,3,4,5,6,7,8	
36		11,12,13					1,2,3,4,5,6,7,8
37	18,19						
38			8,9,10,11				
39	19,20	12,13,14			4,5,6,7,8,9		
40				6,7,8,9,10			

Some observations:

- 1, 2, 4, 8, 16, 32 . . . (powers of 2) cannot be expressed as the sum of consecutive numbers.
- All odd numbers except 1 can be expressed as the sum of 2 consecutive numbers.
- All multiples of 3 except 3 can be expressed as the sum of 3 consecutive numbers.
- All multiples of 5 except 5 and 10 can be expressed as the sum of 5 consecutive numbers.

(Note that this investigation excludes zero.)

PE purchases: extended tables

(Lesson 16)

To be satisfied that there are no other possible solutions to the problems, the tables need to be extended to include all possible sums up to £40, and all pairs of numbers across the tables need to be checked for sums of £27 or £40.

Here are the extended tables:

balls and hoops (number of each)	cost
1	£3.75
2	£7.50
3	£11.25
4	£15
5	£18.75
6	£22.50
7	£26.25
8	£30
9	£33.75
10	£37.50

number of PE mats	cost
1	£2.75
2	£5.50
3	£8.25
4	£11
5	£13.75
6	£16.50
7	£19.25
8	£22
9	£24.75
10	£27.50
11	£30.25
12	£33
13	£35.75
14	£38.50

There are no other pairs of amounts with sums of £27 or £40, so there is only one solution for each problem.

Dog run: all possibilities

(Lesson 18)

Here are all the possible triangles or quadrilaterals for problems 1, 2 and 4. The list for problem 3 is shown in the **Plenary** for Lesson 18.

- **Problem 1**

  4 triangles:

  ABC ABD ACD BCD

- **Problem 2**

  10 triangles:
  ABC
  ABD
  ABE
  ACD   BCD
  ACE   BCE
  ADE   BDE   CDE

- **Problem 4**

  35 quadrilaterals:
  ABCD
  ABCE
  ABCF
  ABCG
  ABDE
  ABDF
  ABDG
  ABEF
  ABEG
  ABFG
  ACDE   BCDE
  ACDF   BCDF
  ACDG   BCDG
  ACEF   BCEF
  ACEG   BCEG
  ACFG   BCFG
  ADEF   BDEF   CDEF
  ADEG   BDEG   CDEG
  ADFG   BDFG   CDFG
  AEFG   BEFG   CEFG   DEFG

Ginger biscuits: some mental methods of calculation

(Lesson 19)

Here are some possible mental methods for solving some of the calculations involved in the problems:

- **Multiplying by 20 (problem 2)**

  One general method is to multiply by 10 and double the answer, e.g.
  $$125 \times 20 = (125 \times 10) \text{ doubled}$$
  $$= 1250 \text{ doubled*}$$
  $$= 2500$$

  * 1250 doubled can be calculated by doubling 1000 (= 2000), doubling 250 (= 500) and adding (2000 + 500 = 2500)

- **Multiplying by 25 (problem 3)**

  One method is to multiply the number by 20 (as above), then multiply the number by 5, then add the two results, e.g.
  $$125 \times 25 = (125 \times 20) + (125 \times 5)*$$
  $$= 2500 + 625$$
  $$= 3125$$

  * 125×5 can be calculated by multiplying 100 by 5 (= 500) and 25 by 5 (= 125) and adding the results (625)

- **69×2 (problems 2 and 3)**

  The 69 could be regarded as 70 and adjustments made, e.g.
  $$69 \times 2 = (70 \times 2) - 2 = 140 - 2 = 138$$

Ginger biscuits: steps for problem 2

(Lesson 19)

Steps for problem 2 on Textbook page 25 are likely to be as follows (although they might be done in a different order):

- **Step 1: Calculate the weight of flour needed**

  $125\,g \times 20 = 2500\,g$ or $2\frac{1}{2}\,kg$

- **Step 2: Work out how many bags of flour the teacher needs to buy**

  2 bags (which hold a total of 3 kg) are needed.

- **Step 3: Calculate the cost of the bags of flour**

  $72p \times 2 = £1.44$

- **Step 4: Calculate the weight of margarine needed**

  $50\,g \times 20 = 1000\,g$ or $1\,kg$

- **Step 5: Work out how many tubs of margarine the teacher needs to buy**

  4 tubs (which hold a total of 1 kg) are needed.

- **Step 6: Calculate the cost of the tubs of margarine**

  $75p \times 4 = 300p = £3$

- **Step 7: Calculate the weight of sugar needed**

  $75\,g \times 20 = 1500\,g$ or $1\frac{1}{2}\,kg$

- **Step 8: Work out how many bags of sugar the teacher needs to buy**

  2 bags (which hold a total of 2 kg) are needed.

- **Step 9: Calculate the cost of the bags of sugar**

  $69p \times 2 = £1.38$

- **Step 10: Calculate the total cost of the ingredients**

  $£1.44 + £3 + £1.38 = £5.82$

- **Step 11: Subtract the total cost of the ingredients from £10**

  $£10 - £5.82 = £4.18$

Multiples and tests of divisibility

(Lessons 20 and 23)

'Multiple of' and 'divisible by' are synonymous terms, e.g. a **multiple of 3** is a number that is **divisible by 3**; a **multiple of 4** is a number that is **divisible by 4**.

Although tests of divisibility are not introduced until Year 5 in the *Framework for teaching mathematics*, more able children may find some of them useful for identifying multiples of numbers, and in Lesson 20, for checking that their lists of multiples are correct.

A whole number is divisible by (is a multiple of):

- 2 if the units digit is even;
- 3 if the sum of the digits of the number is divisible by 3, e.g. 48 is divisible by 3 because $4 + 8 = 12$, which is divisible by 3;
- 4 if the last two digits are divisible by 4;
- 5 if the units digit is 0 or 5;
- 6 if the number is divisible by 2 and 3 (so an even number for which the sum of the digits is divisible by 3);
- 9 if the sum of the digits is divisible by 9, e.g. 594 is divisible by 9 because $5 + 9 + 4 = 18$, which is divisible by 9;
- 10 if the units digit is 0.

Generating sequences using a calculator

(Lesson 20)

To extend sequences considerably, children could use the constant function of a calculator. Ways of using the constant function vary from calculator to calculator. One common method of generating multiples of 7, for example, is to enter $\boxed{+}\,\boxed{7}\,\boxed{=}$. Now each time $\boxed{=}$ is pressed the next multiple of 7 is generated (7, 14, 21, 28 . . .).

(If this doesn't work with your calculator, then try $\boxed{7}\,\boxed{+}\,\boxed{=}$ or $\boxed{7}\,\boxed{+}\,\boxed{+}$, experiment, or refer to the instructions for your particular calculator on how to activate the constant function.)

The constant function can also be used to repeatedly add a number to a starting number. For example, to start with 7 and then successively add 5, enter $\boxed{7}\,\boxed{+}\,\boxed{5}\,\boxed{=}$. Now each time $\boxed{=}$ is pressed, 5 is added (7, 12, 17, 22 . . .).

Quick time: alternative plenary focusing on problem 3

(Lesson 22)

First ask children to say what time it will be when the clock next shows the correct time and to explain why. (12 o'clock because it is only when the clock has gained 12 hours that the correct time and the time shown by the clock look the same; at all other times the clock is 'ahead'.)

There are two likely methods of solution:

- Listing days and times shown by the clock at noon each day until 12 o'clock appears again is too long a process. A quicker alternative is to reason that as there are 6 blocks of 10 minutes in an hour then the clock gains 1 hour every 6 days. So every 6th day could be listed, showing the displayed time advanced by 1 hour at noon of each day.

  Children will need to know the number of days in March (31) and April (30) when they cross the month boundaries. (See page 95 for help in remembering how many days there are in each month.)

noon on	March 1st	7th	13th	19th	25th	31st	April 6th	12th	18th	24th	30th	May 6th	12th
clock time	12:00	1:00	2:00	3:00	4:00	5:00	6:00	7:00	8:00	9:00	10:00	11:00	12:00

- The clock will show 12 o'clock at noon on 12th May.
- Reason that as there are 6 blocks of 10 minutes in each hour, the clock will show an advance of 1 hour every 6 days. An advance of 12 hours would occur at the end of $6 \times 12 = 72$ days. Discuss methods of calculating on what date this would occur, e.g. 30 days from the 1st March takes us to noon 31st March; another 30 days takes us to 30th April; there are 12 days remaining which take us to noon on 12th May.

Days in a month

(Lesson 22)

To help children remember the number of days in each month, they may find it helpful to learn this poem:

> 30 days hath September,
> April, June and November.
> All the rest have 31,
> except in February alone
> which has but 28 days clear
> and 29 in each leap year.

The 'knuckle' method may also be useful:

Make a fist with either hand. Starting with January, say the months while you tap the knuckles and 'dips' on your fist. The 'knuckle' months have 31 days. The 'dip' months have 30 days (except for February which has 28 or 29).

Winning totals: solution tables and patterns

(Lesson 23)

Here is the table for problem 1 from the **Plenary**.

number of 5s	9	8	7	6	5	4	3	2	1	0
number of 3s	1			6			11			16
winning score of 48?	✔	✗	✗	✔	✗	✗	✔	✗	✗	✔

For the winning combinations of darts for 48, the number of 5s decreases by 3 (9, 6, 3, 0), while the number of 3s increases by 5 (1, 6, 11, 16).

This is because the decrease of 3 fives (15) each time can be counteracted by an increase of 5 threes (15) to produce the same total.

A similar pattern can be observed in a completed table for problem 2 (winning score 58).

number of 7s	8	7	6	5	4	3	2	1	0
number of 3s		3			10			17	
winning score of 58?	✗	✔	✗	✗	✔	✗	✗	✔	✗

Here, for the winning combinations of darts for 58, the number of 7s decreases by 3 (7, 4, 1), while the number of 3s increases by 7 (3, 10, 17).

This is because the decrease of 3 sevens (21) each time can be counteracted by an increase of 7 threes (21) to produce the same total.

Colourful cars: calculating the scale using ideas of ratio and proportion

(Lesson 24)

In problem 2, once children have identified that the tallest bar represents 75 cars, and that this in turn is represented by 15 divisions on the vertical axis, they need to work out what each division on the axis represents.

This can be done through trial and improvement as described in the **Plenary** for the lesson. It can also be calculated using ideas of ratio and proportion, which children should be starting to use in Year 4 and of which more able children may have an instinctive understanding. Here are two methods that could have been employed:

15 divisions represent 75 cars.
So $(15 \div 3 =)$ 5 divisions represent $(75 \div 3 =)$ 25 cars.
If 5 divisions represent 25 cars, then 1 division represents $25 \div 5 = 5$ cars.

More directly, if 15 divisions represent 75 cars, then 1 division represents $75 \div 15 = 5$ cars.

One method children could use to calculate $75 \div 15$ is to count up in 15s to 75 (15, 30, 45, 60, 75) keeping a tally of the number of 15s (5).

Test ramp: a possible approach

(Lesson 25)

Here is one route through the problem, using the second set of results as an example:

- **Using clue B**

  The only pair of distances with a difference of $\frac{1}{2}$ m (50 cm) are 1 m 80 cm and 1 m 30 cm.

  So David's car travelled 1 m 80 cm and Emily's car travelled 1 m 30 cm.

- **Using clue C**

  If David's car travelled 1 m 80 cm (180 cm) then Meena's car travelled
  $\frac{1}{3}$ of 180 cm = 180 cm ÷ 3 = 60 cm.

- **Using clue D**

  If Emily's car travelled 1 m 30 cm (130 cm) then Hannah's car travelled 130 cm ÷ 2 = 65 cm.

There are only two names and two distances left: Jake and Josh and 1 m 55 cm and 2 m 20 cm.

- **Using clue A**

  We know that Jake's distance is equal to the total distance for Josh and Hannah. So Jake's distance must be greater than Josh's distance. So Jake's car must have travelled 2 m 20 cm and Josh's car must have travelled 1 m 55 cm.

The Pizza Place: an algebraic approach

(Lesson 26)

Once it has been established that there are 24 seats altogether at the three tables, the following algebraic approach could be used. In this approach the word 'some' is used instead of the usual algebraic '*x*' (or some other letter). It is an approach that many children will understand.

Let's suppose that the smallest table seats 'some' people.
Then the middle table seats 2 lots of 'some'.
And the biggest table seats 3 lots of 'some'.
So between them the three tables seat 1 + 2 + 3 = 6 lots of 'some'.

The restaurant seats 24 people, so 6 lots of 'some' equals 24.
So 1 'some' equals 24 ÷ 6 = 4

So 4 people can sit at the smallest table.
$2 \times 4 = 8$ people can sit at the middle table.
$3 \times 4 = 12$ people can sit at the biggest table.

Finding equivalent fractions using fraction walls

(Lesson 30)

Fraction walls are useful for determining equivalent fractions. Here are some examples:

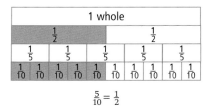

$$\frac{5}{10} = \frac{1}{2}$$

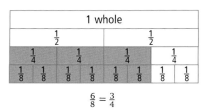

$$\frac{6}{8} = \frac{3}{4}$$

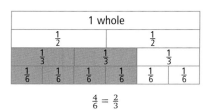

$$\frac{4}{6} = \frac{2}{3}$$

Animal farm 1

Half of the animals in a field are sheep. The rest are geese.

There are 42 legs altogether. How many sheep are there?

Forget the legs to start with.
How many sheep and geese
could there be? Investigate.
For example:
1 sheep and 1 goose
2 sheep and 2 geese . . .

Animal farm 2

One third of the animals in a field are cows.
The rest are turkeys.

There are 48 legs altogether. How many turkeys
are there?

Forget the legs to start with.
How many cows and turkeys
could there be? Investigate.

Animal farm 3

One eighth of the animals in a field are goats. The rest are chickens.

There are 108 legs altogether. How many chickens are there?

Money bags

1 Ravi divided 7 pennies among 3 money bags.

He could then pay any amount of money from 1p to 7p just by giving bags.

How many pennies did Ravi put in each bag?

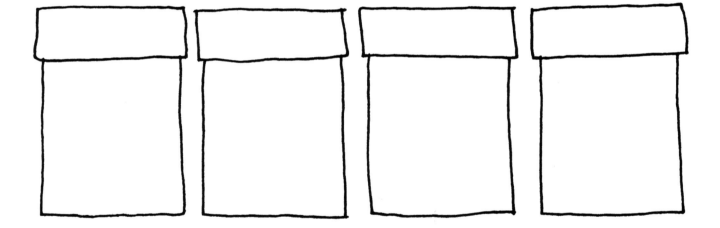

2 Jenny divided 15 pennies among 4 money bags.

She could then pay any amount from 1p to 15p just by giving bags.

How many pennies did Jenny put in each bag?

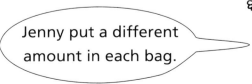

Jenny put a different amount in each bag.

Number line race

Fred Frog, Freda Frog and Francis Frog are playing a game on a number line.

Fred starts at 1. He jumps in 2s.

Freda starts at –19. She jumps in 4s.

Francis starts at –20. He jumps in 3s.

All frogs jump at the same time.

Which frog reaches 25 first?

How many jumps behind are each of the other frogs?

You might find it helpful to complete this table.

	jump														
starting number	1	2	3	4	5	6	7	8	9	10	11	12	13	14	15
Fred	1														
Freda	–19														
Francis	–20														

Fair shares 1

Ben has $\frac{1}{4}$ the number of sweets that Amy has.

Amy doesn't think that is very fair.

She gives 12 of her sweets to Ben.

Now they each have the same number of sweets.

How many sweets did they each start with?

Fair shares 2

Ben has $\frac{2}{3}$ the number of sweets that Amy has.

Amy doesn't think that is very fair.

She gives 6 of her sweets to Ben.

Now they each have the same number of sweets.

How many sweets did they each start with?

If you know **one** third ($\frac{1}{3}$) of a number you should be able to work out **two** thirds ($\frac{2}{3}$).

Puzzling symbols

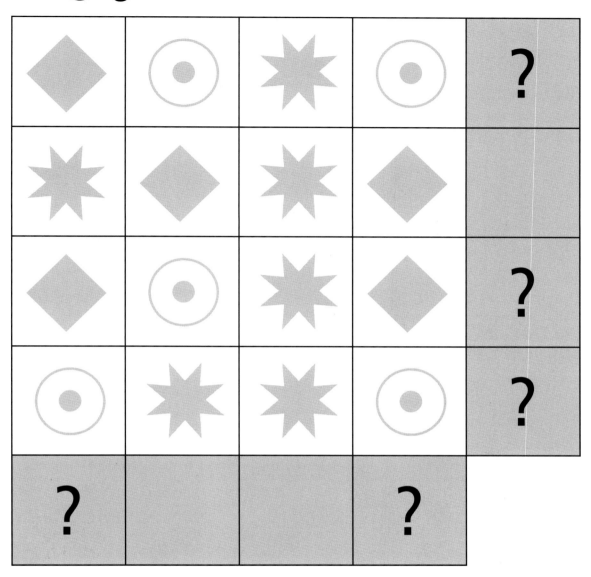

Puzzling symbols: clues

1 Look at the column of 4 ✳s. Work out what ✳ must stand for.

2 Look at the 2nd row down.

Now you know what ✳ is, can you work out what ◆ is?

Secret code

This secret code uses shaded flags to stand for letters.

Some of the flags have not been shaded yet.

Try to work out the code.

1 Shade the blank flags correctly:

  A
 B
 C
 D
E

 F
 G
 H
 I
 J

 K
 L
 M
 N
 O

 P
 Q
 R
 S
 T

 U
 V
 W
 X
Y

 Z

2 Work out what this word is:

         !

_____ !

Secret code: letter blanks

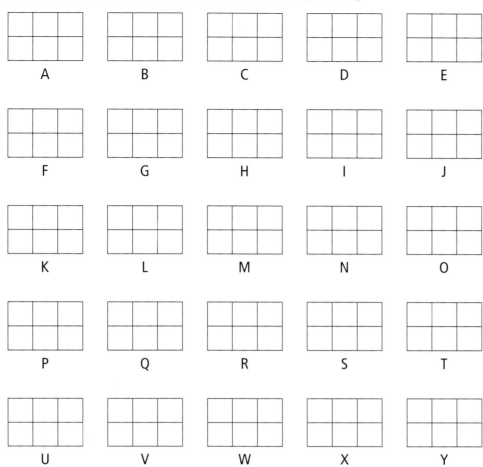

A B C D E

F G H I J

K L M N O

P Q R S T

U V W X Y

Z

Secret code: clues

- Try to work out what all the letters of the alphabet are first.
- You have already been given A. Here are some more letters:

  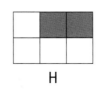 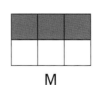 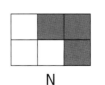

C G H M N T

Hundred square

1	2	3	4	5	6	7	8	9	10
11	12	13	14	15	16	17	18	19	20
21	22	23	24	25	26	27	28	29	30
31	32	33	34	35	36	37	38	39	40
41	42	43	44	45	46	47	48	49	50
51	52	53	54	55	56	57	58	59	60
61	62	63	64	65	66	67	68	69	70
71	72	73	74	75	76	77	78	79	80
81	82	83	84	85	86	87	88	89	90
91	92	93	94	95	96	97	98	99	100

Hundred square

1	2	3	4	5	6	7	8	9	10
11	12	13	14	15	16	17	18	19	20
21	22	23	24	25	26	27	28	29	30
31	32	33	34	35	36	37	38	39	40
41	42	43	44	45	46	47	48	49	50
51	52	53	54	55	56	57	58	59	60
61	62	63	64	65	66	67	68	69	70
71	72	73	74	75	76	77	78	79	80
81	82	83	84	85	86	87	88	89	90
91	92	93	94	95	96	97	98	99	100

Windows 1

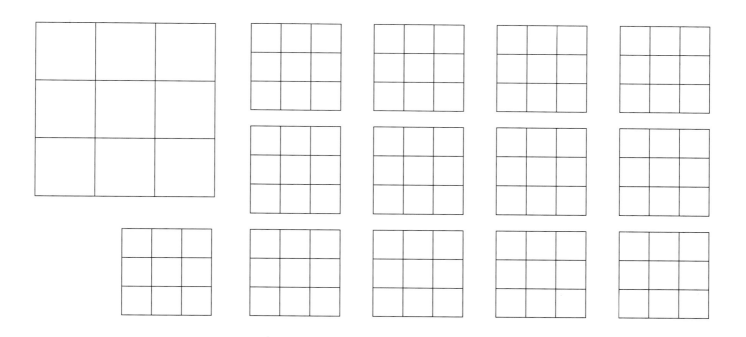

Windows 2

PE purchases

Mr Fitman the PE teacher buys balls,
PE mats and hoops.

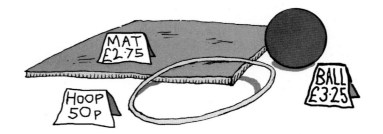

1 Complete each table to show the cost of different numbers of each item:

a

number of hoops	1	2	3	4	5
cost					

b

number of balls	1	2	3	4	5
cost					

c

number of PE mats	1	2	3	4	5
cost					

2 Use the tables to work out the cost of:

a 1 hoop and 1 ball

b 3 hoops and 3 balls

c 1 ball and 1 PE mat

d 3 balls and 3 PE mats

e 2 balls, 4 hoops and 4 PE mats

Apex Maths 4   © Cambridge University Press 2003

PE purchases: clues

What is the cost of:

- 1 ball and 1 hoop?
- 2 balls and 2 hoops?
- 3 balls and 3 hoops? …

How much do 1, 2, 3, 4 … PE mats cost?

Apex Maths 4   © Cambridge University Press 2003

Wristbands

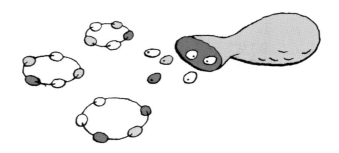

Jack has a bag of beads to make wristbands.

Complete these tables to show how many beads Jack would use for different numbers of wristbands:

1 2 beads on each wristband

wristbands	1	2	3	4	5	6	7	8	9	10	11	12	13	14	15
beads	2	4	6												

2 3 beads on each wristband

wristbands	1	2	3	4	5	6	7	8	9	10	11	12	13	14	15
beads	3	6													

3 5 beads on each wristband

wristbands	1	2	3	4	5	6	7	8	9	10	11	12	13	14	15
beads															

4 Jack has fewer than 40 beads in his bag.

To use up all the beads and have none left over he could make:

wristbands all with 2 beads on
　　or
wristbands all with 3 beads on
　　or
wristbands all with 5 beads on.

How many beads are in the bag? ☐ beads

Use the tables
to help you.

Name .... Date ....

12

Winning totals

On this dartboard there are just two numbers.
You can use as many darts as you like.

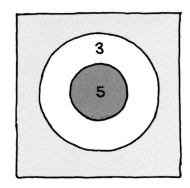

1 Show what scores you could get if all the darts landed in the 5 ring:

darts	0	1	2	3	4	5	6	7	8	9	10	11	12
scores	0	5	10										

2 Show what scores you could get if all the darts landed in the 3 ring:

darts	0	1	2	3	4	5	6	7	8	9	10	11	12
scores	0	3	6										

> You could make a score of 19 with
> 2 darts in the 5 ring and 3 darts in the 3
> ring.
> Use the tables to check!

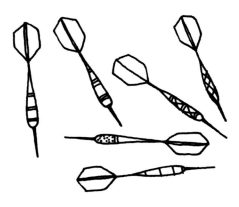

3 Show how you could make these scores:

a 13 _____

b 26 _____

c 38 _____

Colourful cars

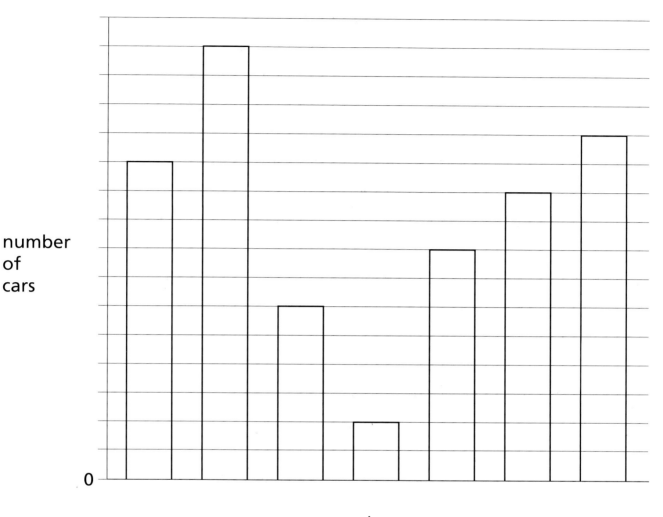

number
of
cars

0

colours

Colourful cars: clues

Which colour has the highest bar?

How many cars does it represent?

Write that number at the same height
as the highest bar on the vertical axis.

Now can you work out all the other numbers for the axis?

Tangrams

Photocopy onto card and cut along the lines.

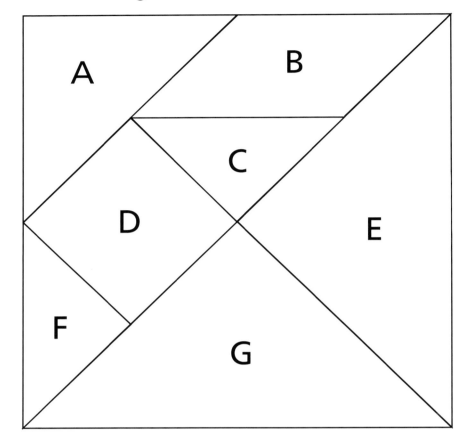

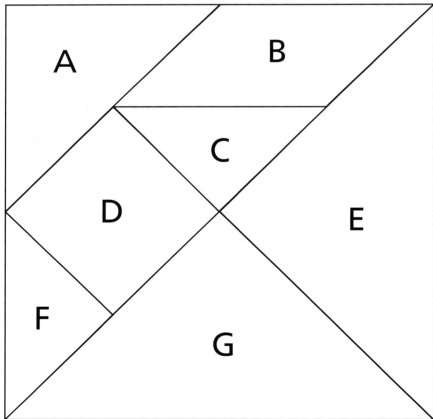

Last digit patterns

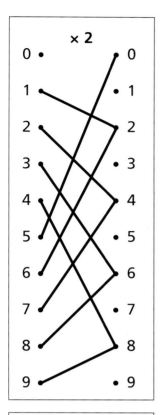
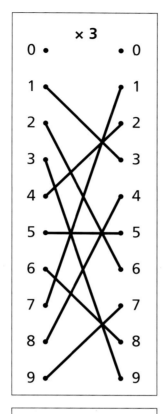
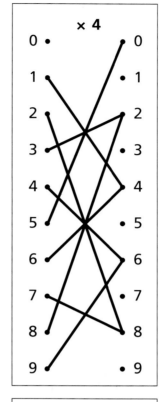
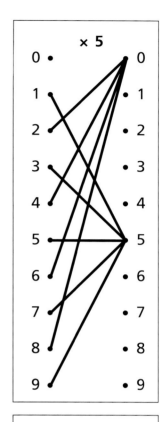
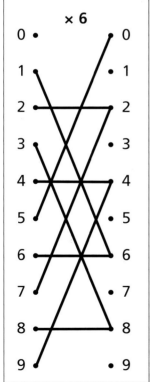
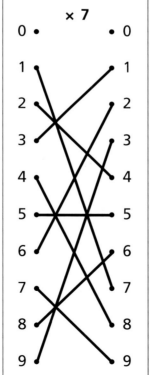
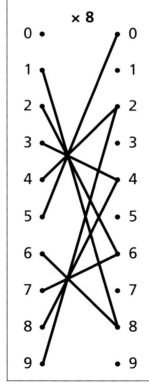
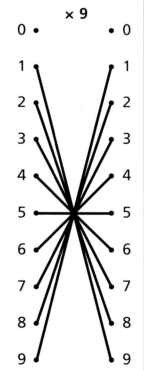

Cutting the cake

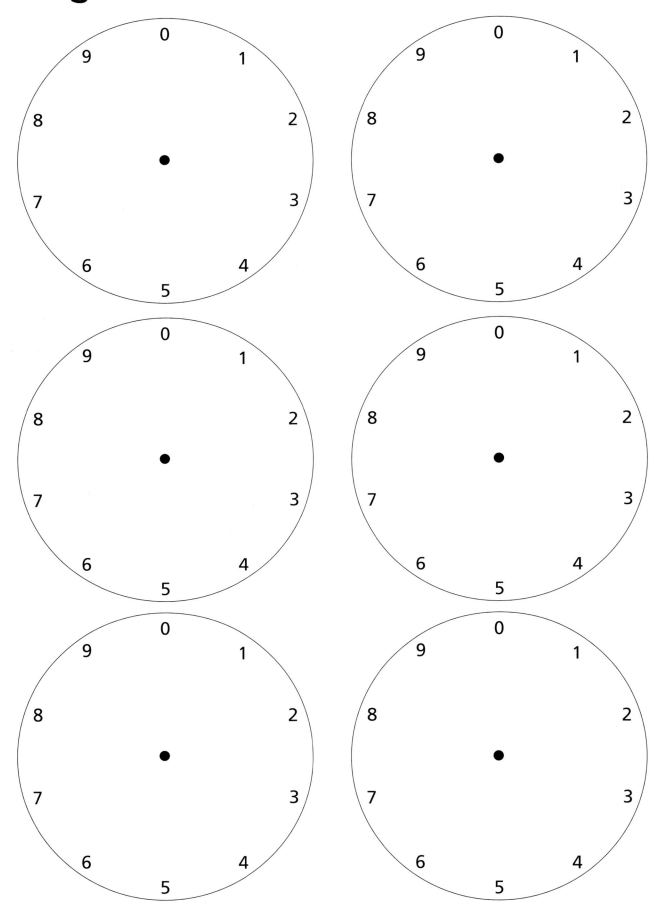